"Allen Klein has a way of authentically bringing the gift of humor to every aspect of life. *The Art of Living Joyfully* reminds you to choose laughter as your companion every day. Don't just buy this book—live it!"

—Terry Paulson, PhD,
author of *The Optimism Advantage*

"Allen Klein has done it again in *The Art of Living Joyfully*! He gives us common sense advice that nourishes joy in all areas of our life. If you are hungry for more joy in your life, then this is a must-have book."

—Susyn Reeve, author of *The Inspired Life*

"Regardless of the situations that life throws at us, Allen teaches us to laugh loudly, love passionately, and live our lives joyfully. Let Allen inspire you to embrace and celebrate the joy in your life and in the life that surrounds you."

—Carole Brody Fleet,
author of *Happily Even After*

"Take these words and love them—take these words and LIVE them!"

—BJ Gallagher,
author of *It's Never Too Late to Be What You Might Have Been*

"The world's only Jollytologist® is the one I turn to when I need jollying. Allen Klein got into the business of joy when he learned the healing power of humor; he has been on the case ever since. *The Art of Living Joyfully* will take up permanent residence on my desk and within easy reach so I can get morning reminders of how to be happy EVERY DAY!"

—Nina Lesowitz,
co-author of *Living Life as a Thank You*

"This powerful collection of quotes serves as a great reminder of simple truths and timeless wisdom that can alter our lives in a profound way. This book is guaranteed to inspire all who read it!"

—Mike Robbins,
author of *Focus on the Good Stuff*

"I use quotations in all my books and presentations. A funny, profound, inspiring quote is a quick way to spice up material. Allen's collection is a great place to find some never-before-seen quotes that will make your communication more intriguing. Read it and reap."

—Sam Horn,
author of *POP! Create the Perfect Pitch, Title and Tagline for Anything*

"Allen, San Francisco Jollytologist®, has been making me happy in a variety of ways since I first met him. I love writing about him for the sheer joy of bringing his presence into my life and recalling all he has to say."

—Janet Gallin,
host of the talk show "Love Letters Live"

mom's
the word

Other Viva Editions books
by Allen Klein:

Change Your Life!
A Little Book of Big Ideas

Inspiration for a Lifetime
Words of Wisdom, Delight and Possibility

The Art of Living Joyfully
How to Be Happier Every Day of the Year

Words of Love
Quotations from the Heart

m o m ' s
t h e w o r d

the wit, wisdom and wonder

of motherhood

COMPILED BY
ALLEN KLEIN

FOREWORD BY
KATE HOPPER

VIVA
EDITIONS

Published in the United States by Viva Editions, an imprint of Cleis Press Inc., 2246 Sixth Street, Berkeley CA 94710.

Printed in the United States.
Cover design: Scott Idleman/Blink
Cover photograph: Tom Grill/Getty Images
Text design: Frank Wiedemann

First Edition.
10 9 8 7 6 5 4 3 2 1

Print book ISBN: 978-1-936740-42-0
E-book ISBN: 978-1-936740-50-5

Library of Congress Cataloging-in-Publication Data is available.

I dedicate this book to mothers everywhere.
For all the love they bring to the world.

C ONTENTS

THERE ARE PLENTY OF MYTHS OF MOTHERHOOD
that still infuse our cultural dialogue about mothers. We
are told that mothers love their children immediately (and
remain besotted), that becoming a mother is the most
natural thing a woman can do, and that in order to be good
mothers we must suppress our own dreams and desires.

I sometimes shy away from books of reflections and
quotations because if their lens is a narrow one, they can
reinforce myths and stereotypes rather than break them
down. This is not the case with Allen Klein's *Mom's the Word*.
Though some reflections do indeed raise mothers up to a
level that is impossible to attain for most women, Klein
doesn't fall prey to reductionism. Instead, he expands what
"mother" means through words from and about all kinds

of mothers. Some reflections are humorous, some loving, some compassionate. Others are brimming with the fear and anger that can also be a part of motherhood. From Phyllis Diller and Erma Bombeck to Ayelet Waldman and Arianna Huffington, there is something in this book for every mother you know.

The words and humor of Klein's own mother also permeate *Mom's the Word* and illustrate the indelible print of mother on child. With this mother as a role model, it's no wonder that Klein is the world's only Jollytologist®!

Mom's the Word celebrates the powerful role that mothers play in our lives and reminds us of the intense joy, frustration, and deep love we experience as mothers. These words honor the mothers we had, acknowledge both the challenges and immense joy of mothering, and ultimately prompt us to reflect on who we want to be in our children's lives. As I dove into these reflections I found myself drawn to my computer with an urge to put my own thoughts about mothers and motherhood down on the page. (Who do I want to be for my children, for myself?) I know you will be equally inspired.

Kate Hopper
author of *Use Your Words: A Writing Guide for Mothers* and *Ready for Air: A Journey Through Premature Motherhood*

INTRODUCTION

PUTTING TOGETHER THE WONDERFUL QUIPS, quotes, and anecdotes in this book has been an absolute joy. The main reason for my delight is that many of them reminded me of my mom, who passed away several years ago at the age of ninety-five.

The quotations about a mother's advice were particularly poignant since I still remember, and live by, the encouraging advice my mother gave me when I experienced a major disappointment in my life. When I was seven-years-old, my parents took me to see both Broadway musicals, *Carousel* and *Oklahoma*. From that day on I wanted to be the person who created "the pretty stage pictures." I wanted to be a scenic designer. Years later, my dream started to come true when I got into Yale Drama School.

It was a three-year master's degree program. I was one of the twelve first-year design students but because they only needed eight students to design their shows the second year, they let go of four people at the end of the first term. I was one of the four to go. I was told I had no talent.

Of course, I was heartbroken. But when I called my mom in tears, she told me that everything always worked out for the best. And she was right. While my fellow students were still in school, I was working at CBS television designing for such national shows as Captain Kangaroo, Merv Griffin, and Jackie Gleason.

The quotations about mothers with positive attitudes are also very meaningful for me since my mom got through life with a strong one. My mom, for example, found some good news in the bad news when she moved to a new apartment. While packing, she had taken too many dishes out of a cabinet and put them on a flimsy folding table. It collapsed breaking half the dishes. When she told me about the incident, she cheerfully noted, "Well, now I have less to pack, less to ship, and less to clean."

And lastly, the humorous quotations throughout the book also remind me of the great sense of humor my mom had. It is perhaps, in part, thanks to her influence that I am in the profession I am today. As the world's only

"Jollytologist®," I teach people worldwide how to have a positive attitude by getting more humor in their life.

I hope you will enjoy reading the words in this book as much as I enjoyed assembling them. I also hope they remind you, if you are a mother, how great you are. Or, how great your mother is or was. This book is a perfect present to yourself, if you are a mother, or for your mother, if she is still around, or for any mother, to say I love you, I appreciate you, I honor you.

Allen Klein, San Francisco, CA
www.allenklein.com

My mother is a poem I'll never be able to write
though everything I write is a poem to my mother.

SHARON DOUBIAGO

A Mother Is...

ACCORDING TO WIKIPEDIA, "A MOTHER (OR MUM/mom) is a woman who has raised a child, given birth to a child, and/or supplied the ovum that united with a sperm which grew into a child."

That may be the accepted definition of what a mom is but we all know that mothers are much more than that. They are diaper-changers and life-changers. They hug us and bug us. They take pride in what we do and take umbrage in what we don't do. They take care of us and are often there for us when no one else is. But most of all, they love us unconditionally.

There are people in this world who spend everyday
making important decisions, troubleshooting,
refereeing fights, nursing egos, doing damage control,
and multi-tasking. They are called mothers.

LINDA POINDEXTER

There is no role in America today that requires
more responsibility, courage and action
than the role of mother.

REED B. MARKHAM

Mothers are really the true spiritual leaders.

OPRAH WINFREY

When God thought of mother, He must have laughed
with satisfaction...so rich, so deep, so divine, so full of
soul, power, and beauty, was the conception.

HENRY WARD BEECHER

An ounce of mother is worth a ton of clergy.

SPANISH SAYING

God could not be everywhere; therefore he made
mothers.

JEWISH SAYING

You know you're a mother
when your child throws up and you run to catch it
before it hits the rug.

ANONYMOUS

Moms are fantastic;
even when they're spelled upside down they're still
WOW!

ANONYMOUS

A mother is the truest friend we have, when trials, heavy
and sudden, fall upon us; when adversity takes the place
of prosperity; when friends who rejoice with us in our
sunshine desert us; when trouble thickens around us, still
will she cling to us, and endeavor by her kind precepts
and counsels to dissipate the clouds of darkness,
and cause peace to return to our hearts.

WASHINGTON IRVING

Mother: The most beautiful word on the lips of mankind.

KAHLIL GIBRAN

Mother is the home we come from.
She is nature, soil, ocean.

ERICH FROMM

Mothers are the most important actors in the grand
drama of human progress.

ELIZABETH CADY STANTON

Mother is the name for God
in the lips and hearts of little children.

WILLIAM MAKEPEACE THACKERAY

Mothers are all slightly insane.

J. D. SALINGER

I believe that always, or almost always, in all childhoods
and in all the lives that follow them, the mother repre-
sents madness. Our mothers always remain the strangest,
craziest people we've ever met.

MARGUERITE DURAS

New mothers enter the world of parenting feeling much
like Alice in Wonderland.

DEBRA GILBERT ROSENBERG

Life is crazy. Now, maybe you knew this all along. But
before I had children, I actually held on to the illusion
that there was some sense of order to the universe....
I am now convinced that we are all living in a Chagall
painting—a world where brides and grooms and cows
and chickens and angels and sneakers are all mixed up
together, sometimes floating in the air, sometimes upside
down and everywhere.

SUSAN LAPINSKI

Even if I'm setting myself up for failure, I think it's worth trying to be a mother who delights in who her children are, in their knock-knock jokes and earnest questions.

A mother who spends less time obsessing about what will happen, or what has happened, and more time reveling in what is. A mother who doesn't fret over failings and slights, who realizes her worries and anxieties are just thoughts, the continuous chattering and judgment of a too busy mind. A mother who doesn't worry so much about being bad or good but just recognizes that she's both, and neither. A mother who does her best, and for whom that is good enough, even if, in the end, her best turns out to be, simply, not bad.

AYELET WALDMAN

Mommies are just big little girls.

ANONYMOUS

Biology is the least of what makes someone a mother.

OPRAH WINFREY

The commonest fallacy among women is that simply
having children makes one a mother—which is as absurd
as believing that having a piano makes on a musician.

SYDNEY J. HARRIS

A mother is a person who, seeing there are only four
pieces of pie for five people, promptly announces she
never did care for pie.

TENNEVA JORDAN

She broke the bread into two fragments and gave them
to the children who ate with avidity. "She hath kept none
for herself," grumbled the Sergeant. "Because she is not
hungry," said a soldier. "Because she is a mother,"
said the Sergeant.

VICTOR HUGO

A mother is a person who if she is not there when you get
home from school, you wouldn't know how to get your
dinner, and you wouldn't feel like eating it anyway.

ANONYMOUS

Where there is a mother in the home, matters go well.

AMOS BRONSON ALCOTT

Mother is the heartbeat in the home; and without her,
there seems to be no heart throb.

LEROY BROWNLOW

Family: A social unit where the father is concerned with
parking space, the children with outer space, and the
mother with closet space.

EVAN ESAR

Mother is the bank
where we deposit all our hurts and worries.

ANONYMOUS

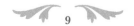

For the mother is and must be, whether she knows it or
not, the greatest, strongest, and most lasting teacher her
children have.

HANNAH WHITALL SMITH

A mother is someone who dreams great dreams for you,
but then she lets you chase the dreams you have for
yourself and loves you just the same.

ANONYMOUS

A mother is she who can take the place of all others
but whose place no one else can take.

CARDINAL MERMILLOD

A mother is not a person to lean on but a person to make
leaning unnecessary.

DOROTHY CANFIELD FISHER

A mother's arms are more comforting than anyone else's.

DIANA, PRINCESS OF WALES

Mothers are the most instinctive philosophers.

HARRIET BEECHER STOWE

One good mother is worth a hundred schoolmasters.

GEORGE HERBERT

The mother is the one supreme asset of national life; she
is more important by far than the successful statesman,
or businessman, or artist, or scientist.

THEODORE ROOSEVELT

You can fool some of the people some of the time, but
you can't fool mom.

ANONYMOUS

You couldn't fool your mother on the foolingest day of
your life if you had an electrified fooling machine.

HOMER SIMPSON

If Father is Pop, how come Mother's not Mop?

GEORGE CARLIN (ATTRIBUTED)

A Mother's Love

ONE OF THE SWEETEST THINGS ON EARTH IS TO watch a mother caress her newborn child. There is perhaps nothing so amazing as the bond of love that exists between them. Yes, there are many other kinds of love—we may love our pets, we may love our spouse, we may love our country, we may even love what we do—but none have the same quality, the same power, the same intense and in-depth connection as there is between a mother and her child.

A mother's love perceives no impossibilities.

BENJAMIN HENRY PADDOCK

Mother love is the fuel that enables a normal human
being to do the impossible.

MARION C. GARRETTY

They always looked back before turning the corner, for
their mother was always at the window to nod and smile
and wave her hand at them. Somehow it seemed as if
they couldn't have got through the day without that, for
whatever their mood might be, the last glimpse of that
motherly face was sure to affect them like sunshine.

LOUISA MAY ALCOTT

As a child my mother always told me, "I am always with
you, right there on your shoulder. And I always will be." I
often find myself in moments of doubt, or concern, whispering to my right shoulder.

BARBARA LAZAROFF

Youth fades; love droops; the leaves of friendship fall;
A mother's secret hope outlives them all.

OLIVER WENDELL HOLMES

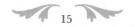

A mother's love is patient and forgiving when all others are forsaking, it never fails or falters, even though the heart is breaking.

HELEN STEINER RICE

The heart of a mother is a deep abyss at the bottom of which you will always discover forgiveness.

HONORÉ DE BALZAC

A mother's love is something we keep locked deep in our hearts, always knowing it will be there to comfort us.

HARMONY FERRARIO

It is not until you become a mother that your judgment slowly turns to compassion and understanding.

ERMA BOMBECK

The angels, whispering to one another,
Can find, among their burning terms of love,
None so devotional as that of "Mother..."

EDGAR ALLAN POE

A mother understands what a child does not say.

JEWISH SAYING

Love your children with all your hearts, love them
enough to discipline them before it is too late…
Praise them for important things, even if you have to
stretch them a bit. Praise them a lot.
They live on it like bread and butter and they need it
more than bread and butter.

LAVINA CHRISTENSEN FUGAL

Loving a child doesn't mean giving in to all his whims; to
love him is to bring out the best in him, to teach him to
love what is difficult.

NADIA BOULANGER

Mother's love is peace. It need not be acquired,
it need not be deserved.

ERICH FROMM

Whatever they grow up to be, they are still our children,
and the one most important of all things we can give to
them is unconditional love. Not a love that depends on
anything at all except that they are our children.

ROSALEEN DICKSON

A mother loves her children
even when they least deserve to be loved.

KATE SAMPERI

Whatever else is unsure
in this stinking dunghill of a world,
a mother's love is not.

JAMES JOYCE

Who is it that loves me and will love me forever with an
affection which no chance, no misery, no crime of mine
can do away? It is you, my mother.

THOMAS CARLYLE

The one thing I never questioned about my mother
was whether she loved me.

LORNA LUFT

Who ran to help me when I fell,
And would some pretty story tell,
Or kiss the place to make it well?
My mother.

ANN TAYLOR

A mother's heart is a baby's most beautiful dwelling.
ED DUSSAULT

A woman has two smiles that an angel might envy,
the smile that accepts a lover before words are uttered,
and the smile that lights on the first born babe,
and assures it of a mother's love.
THOMAS CHANDLER HALIBURTON

There is no friendship, no love,
like that of the mother for the child.
HENRY WARD BEECHER

To a child's ear, "mother" is magic in any language.
ARLENE BENEDICT

One thing about having a baby is that each step of the way you simply cannot imagine loving him any more than you already do, because you are bursting with love, loving as much as you are humanly capable of—and then you do, you love him even more.

ANNE LAMOTT

I always wanted children, but not until they were actually
part of my life did I realize that I could love that fiercely,
or get that angry.

COKIE ROBERTS

I knew that I would love my child, but I had no idea it
would fill me with such a sense of completion.

ROSIE O'DONNELL

I saw pure love when my son looked at me,
and I knew that I had to make a good life
for the two of us.

SUZANNE SOMERS

I used to be a reasonably careless and adventurous
person before I had children; now I am morbidly
obsessed by seatbelts and constantly afraid that low-flying
aircraft will drop on my children's school.

MARGARET DRABBLE

I must trust the world to be kind
to my children, and when it's not,
I will be there waiting with open arms.

TRICIA LaVOICE

Why do mothers have big aprons?
To cover the faults of their children.
JEWISH SAYING

The real religion of the world comes from woman much
more than from men—from mothers most of all, who
carry the key of our souls in their bosoms.
OLIVER WENDELL HOLMES

Mother is food; she is love; she is warmth; she is earth.
To be loved by her means to be alive, to be rooted,
to be at home.
ERICH FROMM

The best medicine in the world is a mother's kiss.
ANONYMOUS

The greatest love is a mother's;
then comes a dog's; then a sweetheart's.
POLISH SAYING

A father may turn his back on his child, brothers and
sisters may become inveterate enemies, husbands may
desert their wives, wives their husbands.
But a mother's love endures through all.

WASHINGTON IRVING

No language can express the power, and beauty, and
heroism, and majesty of a mother's love. It shrinks not
where man cowers, and grows stronger where man faints,
and over wastes of worldly fortunes sends the radiance of
its quenchless fidelity like a star.

EDWIN HUBBELL CHAPIN

Anyone who thinks mother love is as soft
and golden-eyed as a purring cat should see
a cat defending her kittens.

PAM BROWN

Some mothers are kissing mothers and some are scolding
mothers, but it is love just the same, and most mothers
kiss and scold together.

PEARL S. BUCK

We say "I love you" to our children, but it's not enough.
Maybe that's why mothers hug and hold
and rock and kiss and pat.

JOAN McINTOSH

There's nothing like a mama-hug.

TERRI GUILLEMETS

A mom's hug lasts long after she lets go.

ANONYMOUS

I was not a classic mother.
But my kids were never palmed off to boarding school.
So, I didn't bake cookies.
You can buy cookies, but you can't buy love.

RAQUEL WELCH

I don't think that all good mothers have to bake and sew
and make beds and wear percale bungalow aprons. Some
of the finest never go into their kitchens at all; some of
the most devoted are also some of the richest.

KATHLEEN NORRIS

My mother's love has always been a sustaining force
for our family, and one of my greatest joys is seeing her
integrity, her compassion, her intelligence reflected
in my daughters.

MICHELLE OBAMA

Mothers are like glue. Even when you can't see them,
they're still holding the family together.

SUSAN GALE

Mama was the greatest teacher, a teacher of compassion,
love and fearlessness. If love is sweet as a flower, then my
mother is that sweet flower of love.

STEVIE WONDER

Fifty-four years of love and tenderness and crossness and
devotion and unswerving loyalty. Without her I could
only have achieved a quarter of what I have achieved,
not only in terms of success and career, but in terms of
personal happiness.

NOËL COWARD

Most of all the other beautiful things in life come by twos
and threes, by dozens and hundreds. Plenty of roses,
stars, sunsets, rainbows, brothers and sisters, aunts and
cousins, but only one mother in the whole world.

KATE DOUGLAS WIGGIN

Mother Nature knew we would all have to say good-bye
to our mothers one day…so she gifted all of her children
with maternal love.

TRICIA LaVOICE

You never realize how much your mother loves you till
you explore the attic—and find every letter you ever sent
her, every finger painting, clay pot, bead necklace, Easter
chicken, cardboard Santa Claus, paperlace Mother's Day
card and school report since day one.

PAM BROWN

A mother's heart is a patchwork of love.

ANONYMOUS

There is an instinct in a woman to love most her own
child—and an instinct to make any child
who needs her love, her own.

ROBERT BRAULT

I think once you're a mother to one,
you're a mother to them all.

SAMANTHA MORTON

Becoming a Mother

I DON'T KNOW WHAT IT IS LIKE TO BECOME A mother—to carry around a human being within you for nine-months and then to give birth to that being must be astounding. What I do know, as a father, is that to even consider bringing a child into this world is a huge commitment, one that could last for a minimum of eighteen to twenty years, and maybe even a lifetime.

As the quotations below reveal, in both a humorous and not-so-humorous way, there is a lot to consider not only in deciding to have a child but also in the trials and tribulations of the pregnancy period, the birthing experience, and dealing with the caring of a newborn baby.

Making the decision to have a child—it's momentous. It is to decide forever to have your heart go walking around outside your body.

ELIZABETH STONE

I want to have children but my friends scare me. One of them told me she was in labor for thirty-six hours. I don't even want to do something that feels good for thirty-six hours.

RITA RUDNER

I can't have children. Because I have white couches.

CARRIE SNOW

A friend asked her doctor if a woman should have children after thirty-five. I said thirty-five children is enough for any woman!

GRACIE ALLEN

How to Know Whether You Are Ready to Have Kids

Grocery Store Test:
Borrow one or two small animals (goats are best) and take them with you as you shop. Always keep them in sight and pay for anything they eat or damage.

Dressing Test:
Obtain one large, unhappy, live octopus. Stuff into a small net bag making sure that all the arms stay inside.

Creativity Test:
Take an egg carton. Using a pair of scissors and a jar of paint, turn it into an alligator. Now take a toilet paper tube and turn it into an attractive Christmas candle. Use only scotch tape and a piece of foil. Last, take a milk carton, a Ping-Pong ball, and an empty box of Cocoa Puffs. Make an exact replica of the Eiffel Tower.

ANONYMOUS

I was asking my friend who has children, "What if I have a baby and I dedicate my life to it and it grows up to hate me. And it blames everything wrong with its life on me." And she said, "What do you mean, *'if'*?"

R I T A   R U D N E R

If you are the fussy, old-fashioned type of person who considers sleep necessary, give up baby raising and go back to raising hamsters.

E L I N O R   G O U L D I N G   S M I T H

Mothers are basically part of a scientific experiment to prove that sleep is not a crucial part of human life.

A N O N Y M O U S

Who was the demented walkie-talkie maven who decided that parents need to hear each little hiccup their kids make? How is a kid going to develop lungpower if every little whimper makes Mom come running? My recommendation: Keep the baby monitor you got as a gift and put it under the guest bed—lots more fun!

C A T H Y   C R I M M I N S

For about a month after my baby was born I bragged
to everyone that I had the perfect baby because
he never cried. Then I realized those baby monitors
have volume control.

FRANCES DILORINZO

The joys of motherhood are never fully experienced until
the children are in bed.

ANONYMOUS

There never was a child so lovely,
but his mother was glad to get him asleep.

RALPH WALDO EMERSON

At the mall I saw a kid on a leash.
And I think if I ever have a kid, it's gonna be cordless.

WENDY LIEBMAN

We've begun to long for the pitter-patter of little feet—
so we bought a dog.
Well, it's cheaper, and you get more feet.

RITA RUDNER

It's so expensive and time-consuming to have a baby;
you might as well keep hothouse orchids.
At least you can sell them.

ANNE LAMOTT

Women are having babies much later in life than a few
decades ago. There are a lot of practical reasons behind
this trend, too. Nowadays, couples need two salaries to
keep up with the astronomical cost of buying homes,
cars, and a Starbucks nonfat mocha latte.

JAN KING

I bought a pig because I wasn't yet ready for children.
I wanted something small and helpless that wouldn't
require college or quality time. I figured if the pig didn't
work out we could always have dinner.
That's not an option with children.

JENNIFER BALL

If I ever have a kid I'm definitely going to breast-feed it.
Because I don't know how to cook. I would be breast-
feeding him through college. His friends will be jealous.

WENDY LIEBMAN

I'll never have a baby because I'm afraid
I'll leave it on top of my car.

LIZZ WINSTEAD

Ask a first-time mother what her due date is
and she'll tell you the exact date.
A second-timer will tell you the month.
The veteran just says, "Spring."

LIZ CURTIS HIGGS

The most effective form of birth control I know is
spending the day with my kids.

JILL BENSLEY

Enjoying pregnancy is like finding pleasure in having
your kitchen remodeled. Sure, it is fun to plan, and in
the end, you get to proudly show off the results to family
and friends. But throughout the job, you're just plain
uncomfortable and the place is never the same again.

JEN SINGER

Advice to expectant mothers: you must remember that
when you are pregnant, you are eating for two. But you
must also remember that the other one of you is about
the size of a golf ball, so let's not get overboard with it. I
mean, a lot of pregnant women eat as though the other
person they're eating for is Orson Welles.

DAVE BARRY

By far the most common craving of pregnant women
is not to be pregnant.

PHYLLIS DILLER

If pregnancy were a book,
they would cut the last two chapters.

NORA EPHRON

Lamaze, Bradley and other natural
childbirth systems reduce pain and enhance
the exhilarating experience of childbirth.
a. true
b. you've got to be joking.

JUDY GRUEN

"Feel the baby kicking, feel the baby kicking," says my friend who is six minutes pregnant and deliriously happy about it. To me, life is tough enough without having someone kick you from the inside.

RITA RUDNER

My husband, bless his little heart, still maintained that I looked like royalty. I stood before him in my ninth month and asked him if he still thought I looked like a queen. "Absolutely," he lovingly answered. "The Queen Mary."

LINDA FITERMAN

I was slowly taking on the dimensions
of a chest of drawers.

MARIA AUGUSTA TRAPP

…everything grows rounder and wider and weirder, and I sit in the middle of it all and wonder who in the world you will turn out to be.

CARRIE FISHER

Co-workers and friends ask the same three questions,
over and over:

1. "When are you due?"
2. "Have you picked out your names yet?"
3. "What do you want, a boy or girl?"

I finally gave up and pinned a sign
to my maternity jumper:

1. July 27
2. Matthew or Lillian
3. Is there a 3rd option?
LIZ CURTIS HIGGS

The only time a woman wishes she were a year older
is when she is expecting a baby.
BARBARA JOHNSON

Think of stretch marks as pregnancy service stripes.
JOYCE ARMOR

A pregnant woman and her husband made their
first visit to the doctor. After examining the woman,
the doctor took a small stamp and stamped her stomach
with indelible ink. The couple was curious about what
the stamp was for, so when they got home, the husband
got out his magnifying glass to see what it was. In very
tiny letters, the stamp said, "When you can read this,
come back and see me."

A N O N Y M O U S

MATERNITY CLOTHES

1st baby:
You begin wearing maternity clothes as soon as your OB/GYN confirms your pregnancy.

2nd baby:
You wear your regular clothes for as long as possible.

3rd baby:
Your maternity clothes ARE your regular clothes.

ANONYMOUS

Once one of my kids said to a neighbor's child, "Let's play pregnant." The other kid said, "O.K.! What do I do?" and my kid replied, "You faint and I'll throw up."

PHYLLIS DILLER

A pregnant woman, with her first child, goes to see her obstetrician. During the visit, she takes the doctor aside and whispers, "My husband wants me to ask you…"
"I know, I know," the doctor says. "People ask me that question all the time. You can do it as much as you want until late in the pregnancy."
That night, the woman's husband asks eagerly, "Well, what did the doctor say?"
"It will be fine, honey.
The doctor said I can still mow the lawn."

ANONYMOUS

How can I have morning sickness
when I don't get up till noon?

RITA RUDNER

"You are the caretaker of the generations, you are the birth giver," the sun told the woman. "You will be the carrier of this universe."
SIOUX MYTH

The birth of every new baby is God's vote of confidence in the future of man.
IMOGENE FEY

Mothers have as powerful an influence over the welfare of future generations as all other earthly causes combined.
JOHN S. C. ABBOTT

There is no influence so powerful as that of the mother.
SARAH JOSEPHA HALE

How beautifully everything is arranged by Nature; as soon as a child enters the world, it finds a mother ready to take care of it.
JULES MICHELET

Was it the act of giving birth that made you a mother?
Did you lose that label when you relinquished your
child? If people were measured by their deeds, on the
one hand, I had a woman who had chosen to give me
up; on the other, I had a woman who'd sat up with me
at night when I was sick as a child, who'd cried with me
over boyfriends, who'd clapped fiercely at my law school
graduation. Which acts made you more of a mother?
Both, I realized. Being a parent wasn't just about bearing
a child. It was about bearing witness to its life.

JODI PICOULT

On the day my twins were born, I got up before dawn,
showered, put on just a touch of mascara, and sat on the
end of the bed to wait…. I remember every detail—
a day like this is lifted from the rest; it stands alone,
etched in light.

MIA FARROW

[My daughter's] birth was the incomparable gift of seeing
the world at quite a different angle than before,
and judging it by a standard that would apply
far beyond my natural life.

ALICE WALKER

I stood in the hospital corridor the night after she was born. Through a window I could see all the small, crying infants, and somehow among them slept the one who was mine. I stood there for hours filled with happiness.

LIV ULLMANN

I think, at a child's birth, if a mother could ask a fairy godmother to endow it with the most useful gift, that gift would be curiosity.

ELEANOR ROOSEVELT

Some women are lucky, you know. They gave birth to babies. I gave birth to teen-agers. Our daughter was born with a Princess phone growing out of her ear. Our son was born with his foot extended in an accelerator position and a set of car keys in his little fist. The third was born hostile. (Even in the nursery he staged a protest to lower the age of birth to a five-month fetus.)

ERMA BOMBECK

I know there are all these new and wonderful birthing methods where you put the baby in water or lay it on your stomach and pour warm mushroom-barley soup over it to ease the poor unsuspecting thing into the real world. I'm in favor of a more straightforward approach to life; I think the delivery room should have traffic noise and pollution, and you should immediately put the baby on the phone and have someone be rude to it. The baby should then have the option to go back in.

RITA RUDNER

People are giving birth underwater now.
They say it's less traumatic for the baby because it's in
water… I guess it probably would be less traumatic
for the baby, but certainly more traumatic for the other
people in the pool.

ELAYNE BOOSLER

I think I'd be a good mother—maybe a little overprotec-
tive. Like I would never let the kid out—of my body.

WENDY LIEBMAN

My mother's version of natural childbirth was…
she took off her makeup.

RITA RUDNER

It sometimes happens, even in the best of families,
that a baby is born.
This is not necessarily cause for alarm.
The important thing is to keep your wits
about you and borrow some money.

ELINOR GOULDING SMITH

Hard labor: A redundancy, like "working mother."

JOYCE ARMOR

When I had my baby, I screamed and screamed. And that
was just during conception.

JOAN RIVERS

Having a baby is like trying to push a grand piano
through a transom.

ALICE ROOSEVELT LONGWORTH

Giving birth is like taking your lower lip
and forcing it over your head.

CAROL BURNETT

I think of birth as the search for a larger apartment.

RITA MAE BROWN

The three most beautiful sights:
A potato garden in bloom, a ship in sail,
a woman after the birth of her child.

IRISH SAYING

Is not a young mother one of the sweetest sights
which life shows us?

WILLIAM MAKEPEACE THACKERAY

Life was diapers and little jars of pureed apricots and
bottles and playpens and rectal thermometers and all
those small dirty faces and all those questions.

PAT LOUD

A baby usually wakes up in the wee-wee hours
of the morning.

ANONYMOUS

A child of one can be taught not to do certain things
such as touch a hot stove, turn on the gas, pull lamps off
their tables by their cords, or wake mommy before noon.

JOAN RIVERS

There are three reasons for breast-feeding: The milk is
always at the right temperature; it comes in attractive
containers; and the cat can't get it.

IRENA CHALMERS

Don't ever tell the mother of a newborn
that her baby's smile is just gas.

JILL WOODHULL

HINDSIGHT:
What Mom experiences from changing
too many diapers.

ANONYMOUS

Isn't that a wonderful title for a new mother?
Chief cook and bottom washer.

ROBERT ORBEN

Ask your child what he wants for dinner
only if he's buying.

FRAN LEBOWITZ

50

In general, my children refuse to eat anything
that hasn't danced on television.

ERMA BOMBECK

Undoubtedly, the first official act of parenthood is
naming the child. Most mothers, and occasionally
fathers, give this a great deal of thought. Some, however,
don't… A countrywoman told me this tale many years
ago. People in her neck of the woods thought it quite
classy to give a child, male or female, a French-sounding
name beginning with "La." But the father was really
furious when he came home from World War II to find
out that his wife had named their daughter Latrine!

MARGARET G. BIGGER

A new baby is like the beginning of all things—wonder,
hope, a dream of possibilities.

EDA LESHAN

Only mothers can think of the future—
because they give birth to it in their children.

MAXIM GORKY

Baby's Name

1st baby:
You pore over baby-name books and practice
pronouncing and writing combinations of
all your favorites.

2nd baby:
Someone has to name their kid
after your great-aunt.
Mavis, right? It might as well be you.

3rd baby:
You open a name book, close your eyes, and see
where your finger falls. Bimaldo? Perfect!

Anonymous

In the sheltered simplicity of the first days after
a baby is born, one sees again the magical closed circle.
The miraculous sense of two people existing only for
each other.

ANNE MORROW LINDBERGH

I can't get over the miracle of giving birth.
It was as if the sun had opened up. I became free.

JANE FONDA

Before you were conceived, I wanted you. Before you were
born, I loved you. Before you were here an hour, I would
die for you. This is the miracle of life.

MAUREEN HAWKINS

There is no other closeness in humans like the closeness
between a mother and her baby—chronologically, physi-
cally, and spiritually they are just a few heartbeats away
from being the same person.

SUSAN CHEEVER

The drama of the birth is over. The cord is cut, the first
cry heard: A new life begun… The Mother—seeing,
hearing, perhaps touching her baby—scarcely notices the
world around her, let alone how much her body aches.
She just participated in a miracle.

CARROLL DUNHAM

I Remember Mama

PERHAPS THE BIGGEST THING I REMEMBER ABOUT my mother was her verve for life and her great sense of humor.

Every Saturday night there would be live music at the facility where my mom lived after my dad died. At every one of those events, mom used her walker as her partner to dance around the meeting room. She even gave it a name: "Fred Astaire."

And my favorite funny story about my mom happened when she was stuck at the doctor's office with no ride home. She was the last patient of the day and the van that usually transports her back and forth to the doctor did not show up. The receptionist said, "Mrs. Klein, I cannot let you wait here, the doctor has an appointment and I need to close the office. But I'll tell you what I can do. I'll take you downstairs. There is pizza place where you can wait. I'll buy you a Coke and call the van service to make sure they are coming."

They did that and my Mom waited and waited but the van never showed up. So my Mom went up to the counter and asked if they deliver. The guy behind the counter said, "We're a pizza place, lady. Of course, we deliver. What do you want to order?"

Mom responded, "I want a pepperoni pizza and I want to go with it."

My mother is a walking miracle.

LEONARDO DICAPRIO

She was a genius, my mother.

SALLY KIRKLAND

My mother's wonderful. To me she's perfection.

MICHAEL JACKSON

Her smile was like a rainbow after a sudden storm.

COLETTE

My mother is an amazing woman. Not only did she manage the entire household, she noticed a gift in each of her kids and instilled confidence in all of us that that gift would take us wherever we wanted to go.

BARBARA CORCORAN

I cannot forget my mother. She is my bridge. When I needed to get across, she steadied herself long enough for me to run across safely.

RENITA WEEMS

My mother always taught me, even my dad, just never
let other people's opinions of you shape your opinion of
yourself. And I never have and I never will.

RUBEN STUDDARD

My mother said I must always be intolerant of ignorance
but understanding of illiteracy. That some people, unable
to go to school, were more educated and more intelligent
than college professors.

MAYA ANGELOU

My mother is probably the wisest person I've ever known.
She's not schooled, she's not well-read.
But she has a philosophy of life that makes well-read
people seem like morons.

GENE SIMMONS

My mother inspired me to treat others as I would want to
be treated regardless of age, race or financial status.

TOMMY HILFIGER

My mother said, "You won't amount to anything because
you procrastinate." I said, "Just wait."

JUDY TENUTA

My mother's love for me was so great
I have worked hard to justify it.

MARC CHAGALL

My mother never gave up on me. I messed up in school
so much they were sending me home, but my mother sent
me right back.

DENZEL WASHINGTON

My mother encouraged it so much. She was so supportive.
Even if as a kid, I would do the dumbest trick, which
now that I look back on some things, she would love it,
she would say that's amazing, or if I'd make the ugliest
drawing, she would hang it up.
She was amazing.

DAVID BLAINE

My mother could do absolutely anything.
She was like Martha Stewart before such a thing existed.

CHERYL LADD

My mother taught me that we all have the power to
achieve our dreams. What I lacked was the courage.

CLAY AIKEN

By the time I was 15,
my mother had turned me into a real clotheshorse.

GLORIA SWANSON

My mother had a premonition and she felt that hair-
dressing would be very, very good for me.

VIDAL SASSOON

I learned more from my mother than from all the art
historians and curators who have informed me about
technical aspects of art history and art appreciation over
the years.

DAVID ROCKEFELLER

I have very happy memories of fairy tales. My mother
used to take me to the library in Toronto to check out
the fairy tales. And she was an actress, so she used to act
out for me the different characters in all these fairy tales.

MIKE MYERS

She was so deeply imbedded in my consciousness that for
the first year of school I seem to have believed that each
of my teachers was my mother in disguise.

PHILIP ROTH

I had a very wise mother. She always kept books that were
my grade level in our house.

BEVERLY CLEARY

I always tell people that I became a writer not because
I went to school but because my mother took me to the
library. I wanted to become a writer so I could see my
name in the card catalog.

SANDRA CISNEROS

My mother told me to be a lady. And for her, that meant
be your own person, be independent.

RUTH BADER GINSBURG

My mother was determined to make us independent.
When I was four years old, she stopped the car a few
miles from our house and made me find my own way
home across the fields. I got hopelessly lost.

RICHARD BRANSON

My mother thinks I am the best.
And I was raised to always believe
what my mother tells me.

DIEGO MARADONA

I think my mother...made it clear that you have to live life
by your own terms and you have to not worry about what
other people think and you have to have the courage to
do the unexpected.

CAROLINE KENNEDY

My doctor told me I would never walk again.
My mother told me I would. I believed my mother.

WILMA RUDOLPH

I was raised by a single mother who made a way for me.
She used to scrub floors as a domestic worker, put a
cleaning rag in her pocketbook and ride the subways
in Brooklyn so I would have food on the table. But she
taught me as I walked her to the subway that life is about
not where you start, but where you're going.

AL SHARPTON

My mother's passion for something more, to write a
different destiny for a dirt-poor farmer's daughter, was to
shape my entire life.

FAYE DUNAWAY

I always tried to make my home like my mother's,
because Mom was magnificent at stretching a buck when
it came to decorating and food. Like a true Italian,
she valued beautification in every area of her life,
and I try to do the same.

RACHAEL RAY

My mother loved children—she would have given
anything if I had been one.

GROUCHO MARX

When a child, my mother taught me the legends of our
people; taught me of the sun and sky, the moon and
stars, the clouds and storms.

GERONIMO

My mother taught me that when you stand in the truth
and someone tells a lie about you, don't fight it.

WHITNEY HOUSTON

My mother taught me to walk proud and tall
"as if the world was mine."

ANONYMOUS

I hope they're still making women like my momma. She always told me to do the right thing. She always told me to have pride in myself; she said a good name is better than money.

JOE LOUIS

My mother used to tell me,
no matter what they ask you, always say yes.
You can learn later.

NATALIE WOOD

She [my mother] was the force around which our world turned. My mother was propelled through the universe by the brute force of reason. She was the judge in all our arguments. One disapproving word from her was enough to send us off to hide in a corner, where we would cry and fantasize our own martyrdom. And yet. One kiss could restore us to princedom. Without her, our lives would dissolve into chaos.

NICOLE KRAUSS

My mother tells this story that when I first went to school,
I thought I was going to help the teachers. I didn't realize
I was going to get educated.

MOON UNIT ZAPPA

My mother told me stories all the time.... And in all of
those stories she told me who I was, who I was supposed
to be, whom I came from, and who would follow me. In
this way, she taught me the meaning of the words she
said, that all life is a circle and everything has a place
within it. That's what she said and what she showed me in
the things she did and the way she lives.

PAULA GUNN ALLEN

My mother has always been unhappy with what I do. She
would rather I do something nicer, like be a bricklayer.

MICK JAGGER

You're not famous until my mother has heard of you.

JAY LENO

Success is when your mother reads about you
in the newspaper.

MIKE NICHOLS

My mother always called me an ugly weed, so I never was
aware of anything until I was older. Plain girls should
have someone telling them they are beautiful.
Sometimes this works miracles.

HEDY LAMARR

My mother was the concert master of the symphony.
Absurdity and eccentricity were not criticized.

MARTIN SHORT

The most remarkable thing about my mother is that for
thirty years she served the family noting but leftovers.
The original meal was never found.

CALVIN TRILLIN

My mother missed having dinner with Lyndon Johnson
because she couldn't find the right hat to wear.
While my father went off to the White House to break
bread with the President, my mother, who's not a things
and stuff person, stayed at the hotel and tried on 10
different hats and missed dinner.

EMILIO ESTEVEZ

Thanks to my mother, not a single cardboard box has found its way back into society. We receive gifts in boxes from stores that went out of business twenty years ago.

ERMA BOMBECK

God bless my mom, she had reverse Alzheimer's. Towards the end she remembered everything, and she was pissed.

S. RACHEL LOVEY

Yes, Mother. I can see you are flawed. You have not hidden it. That is your greatest gift to me.

ALICE WALKER

My mother always told me, even if a song has been done a thousand times, you can still bring something of your own to it. I'd like to think I did that.

ETTA JAMES

My mother had a beautiful, soothing voice that made me melt.

GLORIA ESTEFAN

There is nothing in the world of art
like the songs mother used to sing.

BILLY SUNDAY

My mom is a never ending song in my heart of comfort,
happiness, and being. I may sometimes forget the words
but I always remember the tune.

GRAYCIE HARMON

In search of my mother's garden, I found my own.

ALICE WALKER

When I stopped seeing my mother with the eyes
of a child, I saw the woman who helped me give birth
to myself.

NANCY FRIDAY

My mother had a slender, small body but a large heart—a
heart so large that everybody's grief and everybody's joy
found welcome in it, and hospitable accommodation.

MARK TWAIN

When mamma smiled, beautiful as her face was, it grew
incomparably more lovely,
and everything around seemed brighter.

LEO TOLSTOY

For when you looked into my mother's eyes you knew,
as if He had told you, why God sent her into the world—
it was to open the minds of all who looked
to beautiful thoughts.

JAMES M. BARRIE

I think my life began with waking up
and loving my mother's face.

GEORGE ELIOT

A man loves his sweetheart the most, his wife the best,
but his mother the longest.

IRISH SAYING

I love my mother as the trees love water and sunshine—
she helps me grow, prosper, and reach great heights.

TERRI GUILLEMETS

All that I am or hope to be I owe to my angel mother.

ABRAHAM LINCOLN

My mother made a brilliant impression upon my childhood life. She shone for me like the evening star—
I loved her dearly.

WINSTON CHURCHILL

I am so grateful for having you for my mother—a woman
of such fine spirit and unlimited devotion. You have been
my inspiration, always, and whatever I am or become, the
credit for all that is good will be yours.

LYNDON JOHNSON

All I am I owe to my mother...attribute all my success
in life to the moral, intellectual, and physical education
I received from her.

GEORGE WASHINGTON

A man may compass important enterprises, he may
become famous...he may deserve a measure of popular
approval, but he is not right at heart, and can never be
truly great, if he forgets his mother.

GROVER CLEVELAND

Your arms were always open when I needed a hug. Your
heart understood when I needed a friend; your gentle
eyes were stern when I needed a lesson. Your strength
and love has guided me and gave me wings to fly.

SARAH MALIN

I have a last thank-you. It is to my mother Celia Amster
Bader, the bravest and strongest person I have known,
who was taken from me much too soon. I pray that I may
be all that she would have been had she lived in an age
when women could aspire and achieve and daughters are
cherished as much as sons.

RUTH BADER GINSBURG

Is my mother my friend? I would have to say, first of all,
she is my Mother, and with a capital "M"; she's something
sacred to me. I love her dearly…yes, she is also a good
friend, someone I can talk openly with if I want to.

SOPHIA LOREN

For all the ways you've helped me grow,
I want to say I love you so.

ANONYMOUS

One of the very few reasons I had any respect for my mother when I was thirteen was because she would reach into the sink with her bare hands—*bare hands*—and pick up that lethal gunk and drop it into the garbage. To top that, I saw her reach into the wet garbage bag and fish around in there looking for a lost teaspoon.
Bare hands—a kind of mad courage.

ROBERT FULGHUM

I stand on the shoulders of countless people, yet there is one extraordinary person who is my life aspiration—that person is my mother, Celina Sotomayor.

SONIA SOTOMAYOR

Your love for your mother is something that you never completely comprehend until you are separated by the miles from her warmth and her wonder.

COLLIN MCCARTY

Call me All-American, but I love Ham and Cheese sandwiches. And not just any old ham and cheese sandwich... My mother's is the best. I've tried many times to make these sandwiches on my own, but it's never the same.

ANDY RODDICK

Mother & Child

FROM THE RELIGIOUS RENAISSANCE PAINTINGS OF Madonna and Child, to the Victorian painter, Mary Cassatt, who frequently depicted the intimate bonds between mothers and children, to the Good Housekeeping magazine covers of the twenties, painters and illustrators have captured the beauty, devotion, and tenderness of a mother and her child. With a pen and ink instead of a brush and paint, the quotations below capture that same special dynamic bond.

There is only one pretty child in the world,
and every mother has it.

CHINESE SAYING

If your baby is "beautiful and perfect, never cries or
fusses, sleeps on schedule and burps on demand, an
angel all the time," you're the grandma.

TERESA BLOOMINGDALE

...there was something so blissful about smelling the top
of a baby's head, like becoming clean and new again
yourself, getting a chance to do it over....

GAIL GODWIN

It's hard to have a dark mood with a gurgling,
delightful, cherubic baby kissing you
and hugging you.

JANE SEYMOUR

What feeling is so nice as a child's hand in yours? So
small, so soft and warm, like a kitten huddling in the
shelter of your clasp.

MARJORIE HOLMES

Here is this baby and he refuses to eat his solid food. ("Solid" in this case is a euphemism for "squishy.") Are you a failure as a parent? Is he a failure as a baby? Is the pediatrician a failure as a pediatrician? *Would* the baby rather have a hot pastrami sandwich?

This brings us to the primary rule of baby raising…. It is the *Golden Rule* of raising babies. *LIE*. Lie to your mother, lie to your sisters and aunts, and above all, lie to all the other mothers you meet on the street. When a newer mother than you asks for your help, tell her you never had the least trouble. *Your* baby just loved his mashed bananas on the first try.

Elinor Goulding Smith

Today, only a fool would offer herself as the singular
role model for the Good Mother. Most of us know not to
tempt the fates. The moment I felt sure I had everything
under control would invariably be the moment right
before the principal called to report that one of my sons
had just driven somebody's motorcycle through the high
school gymnasium.

MARY KAY BLAKELY

If the world never knows your name, that's alright…
your kids do…and it's "Mom."

LINDA POINDEXTER

When she comes and looks in my face and calls me
"mother," indeed I truly am a mother.

EMMA HAMILTON

Romance fails us—and so do friendships—but the relationship of mother and child remains indelible and inde-
structible—the strongest bond on earth.

THEODOR REIK

My mother taught me to walk proud and tall
"as if the world was mine."

ANONYMOUS

In my previous life I was a civil attorney.
At one point I truly believed that was what I wanted to
be—but that was before I'd been handed a fistful of
crushed violets from a toddler. Before I understood that
the smile of a child is a tattoo: indelible art.

JODI PICOULT

Everybody knows that a good mother gives her children
a feeling of trust and stability. She is their earth….
Only to touch her skirt or her sleeve makes a troubled
child feel better.

KATHARINE BUTLER HATHAWAY

In a child's eyes, a mother is a goddess. She can be
glorious or terrible, benevolent or filled with wrath, but
she commands love either way. I am convinced that this is
the greatest power in the universe.

N. K. JEMISIN

A Mother always has to think twice,
once for herself and once for her child.

S O P H I A   L O R E N

Sweater, n.: garment worn by child
when its mother is feeling chilly.

A M B R O S E   B I E R C E

There are only two things a child will share willingly—
communicable diseases and its mother's age.

B E N J A M I N   S P O C K

Oh, to be only half as wonderful as my child thought
I was when he was small, and only half as stupid as my
teen-ager now thinks I am.

R E B E C C A   R I C H A R D S

My mother finally admitted in her later years that the
easiest way for her to get me to do something was to
forbid me to do it.

G E N E   P E R R E T

Julia, the mother of six children, and Samantha,
who had four, were discussing family life. "I've been
meaning to ask you, Julia," Samantha said, "how in the
world do you manage to get our children's attention as
well as you do?" "Nothing to it," answered Julia,
"I just sit down and look comfortable."

ALLEN KLEIN

I practiced making faces in the mirror and it would drive
my mother crazy. She used to scare me by saying that I
was going to see the devil if I kept looking in the mirror.
That fascinated me even more, of course.

JIM CARREY

Children are the anchors of a mother's life.

SOPHOCLES

Children and mothers never truly part—
Bound in the beating of each other's heart.

CHARLOTTE GRAY

The tie that links mother and child is of such pure and
immaculate strength as to be never violated.

WASHINGTON IRVING

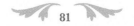

No one in the world can take the place of your mother.
Right or wrong, from her viewpoint you are always right.
She may scold you for little things,
but never for the big ones.

HARRY S. TRUMAN

Even today, well-brought-up English girls are taught by
their mothers to boil all veggies for at least a month and
a half, just in case one of the dinner guests turns up
without his teeth.

CALVIN TRILLIN

The relationship between mothers and children never
changes, and that's because no matter how rich or
powerful you are your mother still remembers when you
were three and put Spaghetti-O's up your nose.

DENNIS MILLER

A mother never realizes that her children
are no longer children.

HOLBROOK JACKSON

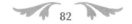

Grown don't mean nothing to a mother. A child is a child. They get bigger, older, but grown? What's that supposed to mean? In my heart it don't mean a thing.

TONI MORRISON

No matter how old a mother is she watches her middle-aged children for signs of improvement.

FLORIDA SCOTT-MAXWELL

You never get over being a child,
'long as you have a mother to go to.

SARAH ORNE JEWETT

A mother has far greater influence on her children than anyone else, and she must realize that every word she speaks, every act, every response, her attitude, even her appearance and manner of dress affect the lives of her children and the whole family. It is while the child is in the home that he gains from his mother the attitudes, hopes, and beliefs that will determine the kind of life he will live and the contribution
he will make to society.

N. ELDON TANNER

Once a child knows that a square millimeter is .00155
square inches, will he ever have respect for a mother who
once measured the bathroom for carpeting and found
out that she had enough left over to slipcover New Jersey?

ERMA BOMBECK

I think that the best thing we can do for our children is
to allow them to do things for themselves, allow them
to be strong, allow them to experience life on their own
terms, allow them to take the subway...let them be better
people, let them believe more in themselves.

C. JOYBELL C.

To nourish children and raise them against odds is any
time, any place, more valuable than to fix bolts in cars or
design nuclear weapons.

MARILYN FRENCH

We spend the first twelve months of our children's lives
teaching them to walk and talk and the next twelve
telling them to sit down and shut up.

PHYLLIS DILLER

A six-year-old and his four-year-old brother were in the
midst of yelling and fighting with each other.
"Children! Children!", exclaimed their frustrated
mother. "Haven't you heard of the Golden Rule?"
"Yes," sputtered the older child,
"but he did unto me first."

ANONYMOUS

Being constantly with children was like wearing a pair
of shoes that were expensive and too small. She couldn't
bear to throw them out, but they gave her blisters.

BERYL BAINBRIDGE

Raising teenagers is like nailing Jell-O to the wall.

BARBARA JOHNSON

I had three children and that's a lot like making a movie.
There are a lot of the same worries. Will it have legs? Will
it go wide? How will it do domestically
and what if it goes foreign?

MERYL STREEP

Sometimes when I look at all my children, I say to myself,
"Lillian, you should have stayed a virgin."

LILLIAN CARTER

I take a very practical view of raising children. I put a
sign in each of their rooms: "Checkout Time is 18 years."

ERMA BOMBECK

Always be nice to your children
because they are the ones who choose your rest home.

PHYLLIS DILLER

Mother's Day

THE HISTORY OF MOTHER'S DAY IN THE UNITED States is, relatively speaking, not a very old holiday. In the late eighteen–hundreds, attempts were made at establishing Mother's Day in connection with promoting peace. It was to honor mothers who had lost, or were at risk of losing, their sons to war. In the years following, those celebrations did not take hold and were sporadic. It wasn't until 1908 that Anna Jarvis campaigned to make it an official holiday. But not until 1914 did President Woodrow Wilson issue a proclamation declaring the first national Mother's Day. And so, on the second

Sunday in May of every year, we continue to celebrate and honor mothers, motherhood, and their place in society.

In addition, we continue to spend lots of money on mom that day. It has become one of the most popular days of the year to dine out. In addition, according to one Internet site, Americans spend approximately $68 million on greeting cards, $1.53 billion on gifts, and a whopping $2.6 billion dollars on flowers. All to simply say "Happy Mother's Day."

Give her a day, and then in return Momma
gives you the other 364. See?

WILL ROGERS

What do you get on Mother's Day if you have kids? You
know what. A card with flowers that are made out of pink
toilet paper—a lot of pink toilet paper. You get breakfast
in bed. Then you get up and fix everybody else their
breakfast. And then you go to the bathroom,
and you are out of toilet paper.

LIZ SCOTT

Mothers stress the lovely meaning of Mother's Day by
gathering their children and tenderly saying, "I carried
every one of you in my body for nine months and then
my hips stared spreading because of you. I wasn't built
like this until you were born and I didn't have this big
blue vein in the back of my leg. You did this to me."

BILL COSBY

The Mother's Day Muddle

1. Your children serve you breakfast in bed
on Mother's Day.
2. They also spill coffee, burn the toast
and wreck your kitchen.
3. You spend all after noon cleaning up.

BRUCE LANSKY

Mother's Day brings back memories of maternal advice and admonition. Picture the scene with these famous offspring.

🌸 Franz Schubert's mother: "Take my advice, son. Never start anything you can't finish."

🌸 Achilles' mother: "Stop imagining things. There's nothing wrong with your heel."

🌸 Madame de Pompadour's mother: "For heaven's sake, child, do something about your hair."

B O B   P H I L L I P S

Spend at least one Mother's Day with your respective mothers before you decide on marriage. If a man gives his mother a gift certificate for a flu shot, dump him.

ERMA BOMBECK

Don't forget Mother's Day. Or as they call it in Beverly Hills, Dad's Third Wife Day.

JAY LENO

Mother's Work Is Never Done

WHEN I GREW UP, THE APARTMENT WE LIVED IN was always clean, there were always clean clothes to wear, and there was always a wonderful home cooked hot meal on the table. As a child I never thought much about how that all happened. If you had questioned me, I probably would have said, "My mom did it," but no one every asked or questioned how all this got done.

Somehow it was expected that mom would do it all. We had no housecleaner, except perhaps prior to a major holiday. We had no "personal chef" nor as many choices for take-out food as there are today. And, we had little money for professional clothes cleaning; there was a washer and dryer in the basement of the apartment building, and that is where mom went to wash clothes once a week.

I rarely saw mom rest. If it wasn't for cleaning and cooking dinner, then mom would be sewing or knitting or baking or making cookies or... Indeed, mom's work was never done.

Mothers are likely to have more bad days on the job
than most other professionals, considering the hours:
round-the-clock, seven days a week, fifty-two weeks a
year.… You go to work when you're sick, maybe
even clinically depressed, because motherhood is
perhaps the only unpaid position where failure
to show up can result in arrest.

MARY KAY BLAKELY

A man's work is from sun to sun,
but a mother's work is never done.

ANONYMOUS

24/7—once you sign on to be a mother,
that's the only shift they offer.

JODI PICOULT

By and large, mothers and housewives are the only
workers who do not have regular time off. They are the
great vacationless class.

ANNE MORROW LINDBERGH

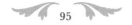

A vacation frequently means that the family goes
away for a rest, accompanied by a mother who sees
that the others get it.

MARCELENE COX

Now, as always, the most automated appliance in a household is the mother.

BEVERLY JONES

I know how to do anything—I'm a mom.

ROSEANNE BARR

Being a full-time mother is one of the highest salaried
jobs...since the payment is pure love.

MILDRED B. VERMONT

You don't have to be a Supermom to succeed
in both your career and child-rearing.
All you need is a $75,000 job and live-in help.

BRUCE LANSKY

It's the biggest on-the-job training program
in existence today.

ERMA BOMBECK

Supermom wasn't a bad job description. The pay was
lousy if you were talking about real money. But the payoff
was priceless in so many other ways.

ROXANNE HENKE

No ordinary work done by a man is either as hard or as
responsible as the work of a woman who is bringing up a
family of small children; for upon her time and strength
demands are made not only every hour of the day but
often every hour of the night.

THEODORE ROOSEVELT

When you're a stay-at-home mother you have to pretend
it's really boring, but it's not. It's enriching and fulfilling,
and an amazing experience. And then when
you're a working mother you have to pretend
that you feel guilty all day long.

AMY POEHLER

If a mother's place is in the home,
how come I spend so much time in the car?

BUMPER STICKER

Forget stay-at-home mom vs. working outside the home mom. I have created a completely biased test of who rules the moms and who the real moms are.

* Real moms never use the bathroom without an audience, no matter the time of month. Her feminine products are found around the house being used to create interesting construction projects.

* Real moms never wax the kitchen floor. Real moms know the only wax that belongs on a floor is from that of a stepped-on crayon.

* Real moms never have conversations without saying the word "potty" or other words associated with private, sometimes embarrassing bodily functions.

VICTORIA CARRINGTON

A suburban mother's role is to deliver children
obstetrically once, and by car forever after.

PETER DE VRIES

I figure when my husband comes home from work,
if the kids are still alive, then I've done my job.

ROSEANNE BARR

There is no such thing as a nonworking mother.

HESTER MUNDIS

All mothers are working mothers.

ANONYMOUS

The phrase "working mother" is redundant.

JANE SELLMAN

Working Mother: Any mother who gets out of bed.

JOYCE ARMOR

If evolution really works,
how come mothers only have two hands?

ED DUSSAULT (ATTRIBUTED)

I'm a single working mom. I have three children, nine
cats, a lizard, a dog and two tadpoles.
I don't go to bed at night; I pass out.

PAULA POUNDSTONE

Child rearing myth #1:
Labor ends when the baby is born.

ANONYMOUS

Who in their infinite wisdom decreed that Little League
uniforms be white? Certainly not a mother.

ERMA BOMBECK

The interesting thing about being a mother
is that everyone wants pets, but no one but me
cleans the kitty litter.

MERYL STREEP

My first job is to be a good mother.

FAYE DUNAWAY

A Mom's Dictionary

Alien:
What Mom would suspect had invaded
her house if she spotted a child-sized creature
cleaning up after itself.

Bed and Breakfast:
Two things the kids will never make
for themselves.

Couch Potato:
What Mom finds under the sofa cushions
after the kids eat dinner.

Anonymous

Tantrums: They are ugly and irritating, and, in public places, can be extremely embarrassing, but sometimes they're the only way to get your child to do what you want them to.

ROHAN CANDAPPA

I looked on child rearing not only as a work of love and duty but as a profession that was fully as interesting and challenging as any honorable profession in the world.

ROSE KENNEDY

Motherhood

IN ENGLISH SPEAKING COUNTRIES IT'S MOTHER, Mom, or Mama. In France, it's Mère or Maman. In Germany, it's Mutter. In Spain, it's Madre, Mamá or Mami. No matter how you say or spell it, the woman who gave birth to you, the female parent, the person who provided care and affection, the person who nurtured you while you were growing up, and the person who mothered you (sometimes overly so), is the person who, according to one writer below, provided "the highest, holiest service to be assumed by mankind."

That service is the service of motherhood.

Motherhood: If it were going to be easy, it never would
have started with something called labor!
ANONYMOUS

Motherhood is not for the fainthearted.
Used frogs, skinned knees, and the insults of teenage
girls are not meant for the wimpy.
DANIELLE STEEL

A mother's life, you see, is one long succession of dramas,
now soft and tender, now terrible.
Not an hour but has its joys and fears.
HONORÉ DE BALZAC

Being a mother is learning about strengths
you didn't know you had, and dealing with fears
you didn't know existed.
LINDA WOOTEN

The story of a mother's life:
Trapped between a scream and a hug.
CATHY GUISEWITE

The motto of a truly heroic mother:
Hang in there, try, fight, fail,
rise up and fight again, and win.
REED B. MARKHAM

Motherhood is still the biggest gamble in the world.
It is the glorious life force. It's huge and scary.
It's an act of infinite optimism.
GILDA RADNER

A hundred years from now…it will not matter
what my bank account was, the sort of house I lived in,
or the kind of car I drove…but the world may be
different because I was important in the life of a child.
KATHY DAVIS

Love is a roller coaster.
Motherhood is a whole amusement park.
CATHY GUISEWITE

Motherhood is like Albania—you can't trust the
description in the books, you have to go there.
MARNI JACKSON

Motherhood is a choice you make everyday, to put
someone else's happiness and well-being ahead of your
own, to teach the hard lessons, to do the right thing
even when you're not sure what the right thing is...and to
forgive yourself, over and over again,
for doing everything wrong.

DONNA BALL

Just being a mother is making me a big, weepy mess.

JESSICA ALBA

Nothing else will ever make you as happy or as sad, as
proud or as tired, as motherhood.

ELIA PARSONS

Sometimes the laughter in mothering is recognition
of the ironies and absurdities. Sometimes, though,
it's just pure, unthinking delight.

BARBARA SCHAPIRO

The only thing that seems eternal and natural
in motherhood is ambivalence.

JANE LAZARRE

Motherhood brings as much joy as ever,
but it still brings boredom, exhaustion, and sorrow too.
Nothing else ever will make you as happy or as sad,
as proud or as tired, for nothing is quite as hard as
helping a person develop his own individuality
especially while you struggle to keep your own.

MARGUERITE KELLY
AND ELIA PARSONS

Being a mother is one of the most rewarding jobs on earth and also one of the most challenging.

- Motherhood is a process. Learn to love the process.
- There is a tremendous amount of learning that takes place in the first year of your baby's life; the baby learns a lot, too.
- It is sometimes difficult to reconcile the fantasy of what you thought motherhood would be like, and what you thought you would be like as a mother, with reality.
- Take care of yourself. If Mommy isn't happy, no one else in the family is happy either.
- New mothers generally need to lower their expectations.
- A good mother learns to love her child as he is and adjusts her mothering to suit her child.

DEBRA GILBERT ROSENBERG

You are a person of the greatest importance when you are
a mother of a family. Just do your job right and your kids
will love you.

ETHEL WATERS

Proving I'm a good mother is the one achievement I'm
most proud of. It's brought out the best in me.

SHEENA EASTON

For me, nothing has ever taken precedence over being
a mother and having a family and a home.

JESSICA LANGE

Motherhood is the greatest thing I've ever done.
This is the greatest thing I'll ever do.

KIM BASINGER

Sometimes when you pick up your child you can feel the
map of your own bones beneath your hands, or smell
the scent of your skin in the nape of his neck. This is the
most extraordinary thing about motherhood—finding a
piece of yourself separate and apart that all the same you
could not live without.

JODI PICOULT

Of all the rights of women, the greatest is to be a mother.

LIN YÜ-T'ANG

Motherhood is the greatest privilege of life.

MARY ROPER COKER

Motherhood is near to divinity. It is the highest, holiest
service to be assumed by mankind.

HOWARD W. HUNTER

Motherhood is neither a duty nor a privilege, but simply
the way that humanity can satisfy the desire for physical
immortality and triumph over the fear of death.

REBECCA WEST

Sometimes the strength of motherhood
is greater than natural laws.

BARBARA KINGSOLVER

Motherhood in all its guises and permutations
is more art than science.

MELINDA M. MARSHALL

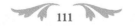

The art of mothering is to teach
the art of living to children.

ELAINE HEFFNER

I am amazed (and secretly delighted) at how many
people stop me to have a look at my baby. Motherhood
seems to break all social barriers as conversations with
strangers of all ages and backgrounds evolve.

SIMON BLOOM

The great motherhood friendships are the ones
in which two women can admit [how difficult
mothering is] quietly to each other, over cups of tea at
a table sticky with spilled apple juice and littered with
markers without tops.

ANNA QUINDLEN

This was an initiation, through which I experienced a
profound kinship with all women throughout history
who had ever gone through this ordeal and transforma-
tion. There was nothing that distinguished me from any
woman who had ever given birth to a baby.

JEAN SHINODA BOLEN

112

While shopping in a supermarket, a woman was pushing
a supermarket cart with a screaming baby in it.
As she went from aisle to aisle, she kept repeating,
"Stay calm, Kathy. Don't cry, Kathy. Don't scream, Kathy."
Another woman watched in admiration and then went
over and remarked, "you certainly have
a lot of patience with little Kathy."
"What do you mean?" snapped the woman. "I'm Kathy."

ANONYMOUS

Thus far the mighty mystery of motherhood is this:
How is it that doing it all feels like nothing
is ever getting done.

REBECCA WOOLF

Though motherhood is the most important of all
professions—requiring more knowledge than any other
department in human affairs—there was no attention
given to preparation for this office.

ELIZABETH CADY STANTON

The toughest part of motherhood
is the inner worrying and not showing it.

AUDREY HEPBURN

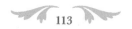

Take motherhood: nobody ever thought of putting it on a moral pedestal until some brash feminists pointed out, about a century ago, that the pay is lousy and the career ladder is non-existent.

BARBARA EHRENREICH

Babies don't come with directions on the back or batteries that can be removed. Motherhood is twenty-four hours a day, seven days a week.
You can't "leave the office."

PAT SCHROEDER

What do you do with all the antennae of motherhood when they become obsolete? What do you do with the loose wires that dangle after eighteen years of intimate connection to your own child? What use is there for the expertise of motherhood that took so long to acquire?

ELLEN GOODMAN

The natural state of motherhood is unselfishness. When you become a mother, you are no longer the center of your own universe. You relinquish that position to your children.

JESSICA LANGE

Don't get so involved in the duties of your life and your
children that you forget the pleasure.
Remember why you had children.

LOIS WYSE

It will be gone before you know it.
The fingerprints on the wall appear higher and higher.
Then suddenly they disappear.

DOROTHY EVSLIN

Mothers & Daughters

MY WIFE DIED AT THE AGE OF THIRTY-FOUR LEAVING me with Sarah, my daughter, who was 10-years-old at the time. Even though Ellen was a gourmet cook, I don't recall Ellen and Sarah being together in the kitchen a lot, nor Ellen specifically teaching Sarah how to cook. Yet, Sarah turned out to be a great cook, has a job as a personal chef with several clients, and a part-time caterer, among other things.

I've often wondered how this happened. How could Ellen's cooking talent rub off on Sarah, particularly since they never had formal cooking time together because of Sarah's young age? And yet, it should probably not be much of a surprise when I consider how close mothers and daughters can be. That's probably how Sarah got her "cooking gene." At least that is what I'd like to believe.

A little girl, asked where her home was, replied,
"where mother is."
KEITH L. BROOKS

There's no question that the mother-daughter relationship is the most complex on earth. It's even more compli-
cated than the man-woman thing.
NAOMI JUDD

My daughters enlighten me about myself. Their presence
acts as a constant, ever-changing reflection of me as well
as a source of feedback, as I see myself mirrored in their
mannerisms, attitudes, and relationships.
ELLEN A. ROSEN

A daughter reminds you of all the things you had
forgotten about being young.
Good and bad.
MAEVE O'REILLY

Kayleigh's mother was lying on the couch, recovering from a virus. Kayleigh [age 4] knew immediately what would make the patient feel better: breakfast in bed.

So she served up her best plastic food, on a tiny plastic plate, and poured imaginary juice in a tiny plastic cup.

"Here, sweetie, drink this," she said as she lifted the cup to her mother's lips.

Touched by her little one's tender care, she managed a smile and said, "Are you going to take care of me like this when I'm an old, old lady?"

"Yes," she said sweetly, "if I still have my toy kitchen."

JUDY MOON DENSON
AND BEVERLY SMALLWOOD

Like most parents Tiffany tells her daughter to "act like a big girl" when she fusses or whines. One day they were wrestling and tickling each other and Tiffany managed to get hit with an elbow in the face. In the spirit of play, Tiffany acted like she was in real pain. Paige, 4, said, "Mom, act like a grown-up!"

GRACE WITWER HOUSHOLDER

Of all the haunting moments of motherhood, few rank with hearing your own words come out of your daughter's mouth.

VICTORIA SECUNDA

The little girl's mother scolded her..."If you don't stop sucking your thumb, you'll swell up and burst." The thought of such a sad ending stayed with her.
A couple of weeks later a friend of the mother's was visiting. The friend was about to become a mother. With her mommy's warning still ringing in her ears, the little girl blurted out, "I know what you've been doing!"

JOEY ADAMS

What I'd like to give my daughter is freedom. And this is
something that must be given by example, not by exhor-
tation. Freedom is a loose leash, a license to be different
from your mother and still be loved... Freedom is...
not insisting that your daughter share your limitations.
Freedom also means letting your daughter reject you
when she needs to and come back when she needs to.
Freedom is unconditional love.

ERICA JONG

When Chelsea Victoria Clinton lay in my arms for the
first time, I was overwhelmed by the love and responsibility I felt for her. Despite all the books I had read, all
the children I had studied and advocated for, nothing
had prepared me for the sheer miracle of her being.

HILLARY RODHAM CLINTON

When my daughter was born,
one of the unheralded joys of motherhood was that I
finally had a legitimate excuse for buying toys.

SARAH BAN BREATHNACH

A young mother was out walking with her four-year-old daughter. The youngster picked up something off the ground and started to put it in her mouth.

"Please keep that out of your mouth," the mother cautioned.

"Why?" asked the little girl.

"Because it's been lying outside and probably has germs," responded the mother.

At this point, the child looked at her mother in total admiration and asked, "Wow! How do you know all that stuff?"

Momentarily stumped, the mother stammered, "Uh, um, it's on the mommy test. You have to know those things to be a mommy."

The pair walked along in silence for a few minutes as the child pondered this new information. "Oh, I get it," she announced excitedly. "Then if you flunk, you have to be the daddy!"

ANONYMOUS

When my daughter was born, we videotaped the birth.
Now when she makes me angry, I just hit "rewind" and
put her back in.

GRACE WHITE

A woman was trying hard to get the catsup to come out
of the jar. During her struggle the phone rang so she
asked her four-year-old daughter to answer the phone.
"It's the minister, Mommy," the child said to her mother.
Then she added, "Mommy can't come to the phone to
talk to you right now. She's hitting the bottle."

ANONYMOUS

The daughter never ever gives up on the mother, just as
the mother never gives up on the daughter. There is a tie
here so strong that nothing can break it.

RACHEL BILLINGTON

A daughter and her mother are never free from one
another—no matter how they disagree. For they are so
entwined in heart and mind that, gladly or unwillingly,
they share each love, each joy, each sorrow and each
bitter wrong lifelong.

PAM BROWN

Dear Mom,

I'm sorry that I haven't written, but all my stationery was destroyed when the dorm burned down. I am now out of the hospital and the doctor said that I would recover soon. I have also moved in with the boy who rescued me, since most of my things were destroyed in the fire. And, I know that you've always wanted a grandchild, so you'll be pleased to know that I am pregnant and it's due in April.

Love,
Mary

Then there was a postscript—

P. S.: There was no fire, my health is perfectly fine, and I am not pregnant. In fact, I don't even have a boyfriend. But I did get a D in French and a C in math and chemistry, and I just wanted to make sure that you kept it all in perspective.

ANONYMOUS

Part of the reason [motherly advice] bugs us as daughters is because our mothers are so powerful in our lives. They loom like giants. The reason mothers keep at it is because they're so powerless. They cannot get you to do what is so obvious to them you should do.

DEBORAH TANNEN

My mother said I drove her crazy. I did not drive my mother crazy. I flew her there. It was faster.
She used to introduce my brothers and me in the following way: "Here is my son, the doctor. Here is my son, the accountant. Here is my daughter—the lesbian."

ROBIN TYLER

If you want to understand any woman you must first ask about her mother and then listen carefully. Stories about food show a strong connection. Wistful silences demonstrate unfinished business. The more a daughter knows the detail of her mother's life—without flinching or whining—the stronger the daughter.

ANITA DIAMANT

I blame my mother for my poor sex life. All she told me was "The man goes on top, and the woman underneath." For three years my husband and I slept in bunk beds."

JOAN RIVERS

"Mommy, where did I come from?", the nine-year-old asked. Her parents had carefully prepared for this moment. They got out the encyclopedia and several other books, and explained all they knew about sexual attraction, love, and reproduction. Then, contented with their response, the young girl's father asked,
"Does that answer your question?"
"Not really," the little girl said. "Alice said she came from Chicago. I want to know where I came from."

ANONYMOUS

There are three books my daughter felt were the most important influences in her life: the Bible, her mother's cookbook, and her father's checkbook.

JOYCE MATTINGLY

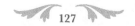

An acquaintance of mine, who is a physician, told this story about her then-four-year-old daughter. On the way to preschool, the doctor had left her stethoscope on the car seat, and her little girl picked it up and began playing with it. Be still, my heart, thought my friend, my daughter wants to follow in my footsteps! Then the child spoke into the instrument: "Welcome to McDonald's. May I take your order?"

HEARTWARMERS.COM

A father asked his daughter what she would like for her birthday. Since her mom was near the end of her pregnancy, the girl said, "A baby sister." Soon after the mother came home with a seven-pound six-ounce baby girl. A couple of months later, the father asked his daughter what she would like for her next birthday. "Well," the little girl replied, "if mom isn't too uncomfortable, I would like a pony."

ANONYMOUS

My then four-year-old daughter had begged for months for me to buy her the "Magic Marvin" markers advertised on an infomercial. I finally broke down and made the call, ordering the markers for her.

About two weeks later, she asked me if I were 18 years
old. I said, "No honey, I'm 38 years old." At that,
she ran into her bedroom, sobbing and crying,
and threw herself across her bed. I ran after her
and asked her what was wrong.
She said that they told her on TV that you had to be
18 years old in order to buy "Magic Marvin" and now they
wouldn't send them to her because I was too old!

HappyFamilies.com

Emma woke from a dream when she was about five,
crying, a bit desperate."I don't know what my husband's
name is and I don't know what my baby's name is!"
This was the kind of funny that wasn't funny for her at
the time but it was so hard not to laugh at the seriousness
given her age. I told her she wasn't supposed to know who
her husband was yet, and as for her unborn child, parents
usually name a child, like her father and I gave her the
name Emma. "No you didn't!" she retorted.
"I was always Emma."

Carol Smaldino

A mother watched as her daughter hopped off the school
bus and scampered toward her house in a pouring
rainstorm. As the little girl ran toward the house, a lightning bolt flashed and the little girl stopped, looked up
toward the sky and smiled, then began running
back toward the house.
Another lightning bolt flashed, and again the little
girl stopped, looked toward the sky, and smiled before
running once more toward the open door of her house.
When the girl finally arrived in the house, her mother
immediately asked about her strange behavior.
"Why did you keep stopping and smiling at the sky?" she
asked her daughter.
"I had to, Mommy," the little girl explained,
"God was taking my picture."

BARBARA JOHNSON

Mothers & Sons

SOME MOTHERS LOVE ROSES, SOME ORCHIDS; MY mom's favorite flower was lilacs. I don't know if it was the purple color, the sweet aroma, or the fact that they appeared in the florist shops every Spring. When I was growing up, and as far back as I could remember, I bought my mom a bunch of lilacs every Mother's Day. Their smell would fill the apartment with a reminder that this was a special time to honor her. And even today, although my mom is no longer alive, I am still reminded of her and past Mother's Days, every time I either smell or see lilacs.

Little did I know then that in the language of flowers, lilacs mean the first emotion of love. Nor that the genus name for lilac is derived from the Greek and means a hollow tube or pipe which, since ancient times was used to make reed pipes or flutes.

So my giving lilacs to my mom, was, in some way, a son's song of love sung to his mother every year.

I've seen my name in letters as tall as a house. I've been
toasted by audiences who've seen me on international
television. I've won virtually every major award my career
offers. I say all of that simply to say this: I've never been
as fulfilled as I was when my son was born.

REBA MCENTIRE

That strong mother doesn't tell her cub, "Son, stay weak
so the wolves can get you." She says, "Toughen up, this is
reality we are living in."

LAURYN HILL

Before my mother would give you that dime allowance,
she'd want you to do a little chore around the house.
Like build a porch.

RAY ROMANO

I was a mother's boy.

DON RICKLES

I can remember the first time I had to go to sleep.
Mom said, "Steven, time to go to sleep." I said,
"But I don't know how." She said, "It's real easy. Just go
down to the end of the tired and hang a left."

So I went down to the end of tired, and just out of curiosity I hung a right. My mother was there, and she said, "I thought I told you to go to sleep."

STEVEN WRIGHT

I would much rather be known as the mother of a great son than the author of a great book or the painter of a great masterpiece.

ROSE KENNEDY

When my son was about four, we visited a friend who was nursing her child. Seeing this, my son came over to me and started to unbutton my blouse. Wanting to explain to him that it wasn't OK to do that and trying to make my point, I gently removed his hand and said, "Sweetie, my body and my breasts belong to ME." Looking at the nursing baby and then back to me, he sadly replied, "Yeah, but they used to belong to ME."

MIRIAM IOSUPOVICI

Miles, [age four], learned the word penis no problem....
But vagina, that was a tough one for him to remember.
In the tub one night he asked what "mine" was called
again. I said, "You know the word, think real hard." I
could see him concentrating, flipping through the small
but growing catalog of words he had mastered. Remem-
bering it was both a "big" word and one that he didn't
use at all that much, he proudly concluded,
"I know—spatula!"

AMY KROUSE ROSENTHAL

There was never a great man who had not a great mother.

OLIVE SCHREINER

I'm very loyal in a relationship, all relationships. When
I'm with my mother, I don't look at other moms, "Wow, I
wonder what her macaroni and cheese tastes like."

GARRY SHANDLING

Happy is the son whose faith in his mother remains
unchallenged.

LOUISA MAY ALCOTT

Mrs. Herman and Mrs. Gerges were talking about their children. "My son" said Mrs. Herman. "Who could ask for a better boy? Every Friday, he eats dinner at my house. Every summer, he makes me spend a month with him in the country. Every winter, he sends me for a month to a hotel in Florida."

To which Mrs. Gerges replied, "I have a son, an angel. For a whole year, he's been going to the most expensive psychiatrist in New York. Every day, month in and out, he goes there. And he talks each day for an hour. And do you know what he talks about, paying fifty dollars an hour?!...Me."

LEO ROSTEN

Erik didn't say a word for the first six years of his life. On his seventh birthday, his mother made him a peanut butter and jelly sandwich.

Erik took one bite and said, "This sandwich is terrible!" His parents were astonished.

"Why did you wait so long to talk?" they asked.

Erik replied, "Up to now everything's been OK."

ANONYMOUS

You have a wonderful child. Then, when he's 13, gremlins carry him away and leave in his place a stranger who
gives you not a moment's peace…. You have to hang in
there, because two or three years later, the gremlins will
return your child, and he will be wonderful again.

JILL EIKENBERRY

With boys you always know where you stand.
Right in the path of a hurricane. It's all there. The fruit
flies hovering over their waste can, the hamster trying to
escape to cleaner air, the bedrooms decorated in
Early Bus Station Restroom.

ERMA BOMBECK

Johnny had been misbehaving and was sent to his room.
After a while, he emerged and informed his mother that
he had thought it over and then said a prayer.
"Fine," said the pleased mother. "If you ask God to help
you not to misbehave, He will help you."
"Oh, I didn't ask Him to help me not misbehave,"
said Johnny.
"I asked Him to help you put up with me."

ANONYMOUS

John invited his mother over for dinner. During the meal, his mother couldn't help noticing how beautiful John's roommate was. She had long been suspicious of a relationship between John and his roommate and this only made her more curious.

Over the course of the evening, while watching the two interact, she started to wonder if there was more between John and the roommate than met the eye. Reading his mom's thoughts, John volunteered, "I know what you are thinking, but I assure you, Julie and I are just roommates."

About a week later, Julie came to John and said, "Ever since your mother came to dinner, I've been unable to find the beautiful silver gravy ladle. You don't suppose she took it, do you?"

John said, "Well, I doubt it, but I'll email her just to be sure." So he sat down and wrote:

Dear Mom,

I'm not saying you 'did' take a gravy ladle from my house, and I'm not saying you 'did not' take a gravy ladle. But the fact remains that one has been missing ever since you were here for dinner.

Love,
John

Several hours later John received a email reply from his mother which read:

Dear Son,

I'm not saying that you 'do' sleep with Julie, and I'm not saying that you 'do not' sleep with Julie. But the fact remains that if she were sleeping in her own bed, she would have found the gravy ladle by now.

Love,
Mom

ANONYMOUS

The best love in the world, is the love of a man.
The love of a man who came from your womb,
the love of your son!

C. JoyBell C.

A mother and her young son were out shopping in the
supermarket. In the laundry supply aisle they followed
a very stout [that means fat] man who was pushing a
shopping cart. The boy was obviously awed by the man's
tremendous size and his mom was becoming worried that
he'd embarrass her by saying something. In fact, she was
so worried that she instructed the boy not to talk unless
it was a real emergency. Just then a beeper on the man's
belt went off, which was enough of an emergency for the
kid. He grabbed his mother's arm and yelled,
"Look out, he's backing up!"

Ron Dentinger

We had been alternating between two CD's—
"Fiddler on the Roof" and Bette Midler—
when Justin, [age six], concocted his first joke:
"Hey, Mom—let's listen to "Bette Midler on the Roof."

Amy Krouse Rosenthal

When my son was in the first grade all he could talk about was getting a horse. One morning when I was taking him to school he started asking me to please get me a horse. I explained to him that a horse costs a lot of money. He looked up at me and said, "But Momma, I don't want a new one I want a used one like the cheap used car you bought!"

ADDIE DAVIS

He is six. He walks into his parents' bedroom and solemnly sets down five copies of his school photograph, which he hates because it was taken when he was toothless.

"Mom," he says, "I know you hate this picture, too, but I think you better keep it. That way, in case I get kidnapped, you'll have something to show the police."

JUDY MARKEY

Just a few years ago, my son came home from school
with a questionnaire from his Family Living Class.
The first question was, "What do you *dislike* about your
parents?" and he had written, "they yell at me." I said,
"WHY THE HECK DID YOU SAY THAT, IT'S EMBAR-
RASSING?!!" The next question was, "What do you *like*
best about your parents?" and I was thinking, "kind,
considerate, fun to be around." But no, what does *my* son
like best about his parents? "They can drive!"

S U S A N   V A S S

Kim told me about her six-year-old son who asked if he
could say the prayer when the meal arrived. Everyone
bowed their heads as he recited the following: "God is
good, God is great. Thank you for the food, and God, I
will even thank you more if Mom gets us ice cream for
dessert, with liberty and justice for all! Amen!"

P A M   V R E D E V E L T

Matthew knows from past lessons that it is impolite to point out differences in public especially by using words like Bald, Fat, Ugly, Funny, etc.

In a recent shopping trip, Matthew and his mother walked into a department store at the local mall. On entering the store, Matthew saw a very large woman in front of them. My wife held her breath praying all the discussions and life lessons we were teaching Matthew would be remembered.

Matthew looked up at his mother and said, "She is big, huh, mom?" "Yes, she is Matthew", she whispered back, hoping that was the end of the discussion. Knowing he mastered another life lesson Matthew proudly stated, "Aren't you glad I didn't use the 'F' word?"

DAVID LEVESQUE

My Mama Done Told Me

I ONCE STARTED TO LIST ALL OF THE THINGS MY mom either directly advised me to do or things I indirectly learned because she did them. I got up to sixty-eight items and then stopped. I'm sure there are lots more if I think about it and someday I might continue that list. But for now, here are a dozen and a half lessons I learned from my mom:

1. Always straighten up the house before the house cleaner comes. You don't want a stranger to see how messy you are.

2. When you are in someone else's bathroom, always wipe the toilet seat before you sit down.

3. The minute you sit down in a restaurant put the rolls that are on the table in a bag. Then immediately call the waiter over and ask for more.

4. At breakfast, talk about what you will have for lunch; At lunch, talk about what you will have at dinner; At dinner, talk about what you will have at breakfast the next morning.

5. Set the table for dinner right after you finish breakfast.

6. At dinner, discuss such major issues as the price of canned peaches at the supermarket.

7. Start all correspondence with "I just want you to know..."

8. Complain about your children; Brag about your grandchildren.

9. Constantly ask why the neighbor's kids are better behaved than yours.

10. Don't write out the check you are gifting a bride and groom, or a bar mitzvah boy, until you determine how much food you got at the reception.

11. After attending a wedding or bar mitzvah, talk about how much money was spent and what a waste it was.

12. Never give anyone a more expensive gift than they gave you.

13. Brag about what your son or daughter does and how important he or she is; Brag about how much money your son or daughter makes; Brag about who your daughter is married to and how much money he makes.

14. Ask everyone you meet, "So what's new?" but never let him or her answer.

15. When someone asks, "How are you?" tell them every pain you have had for the last five years.

16. Whenever someone tells you what he or she paid for something, tell him or her you paid less.

17. Always ask for your senior discount.

18. Ask for your senior discount even if you aren't a senior yet. (Close enough counts.)

When your mother asks, "Do you want a piece of advice?"
it is a mere formality. It doesn't matter if you answer yes
or no. You're going to get it anyway.

ERMA BOMBECK

Just say no.

NANCY REAGAN

Upset with Justin…I said, "Justin, sit down,
I want to give you some advice." After my blabbing and
blabbing and admonishing and blabbing…
Justin very graciously asked, "Can I now have that thing
you said you wanted to give me?"

AMY KROUSE ROSENTHAL

Mother always said that honesty was the best policy,
and money isn't everything. She was wrong about
other things too.

GERALD BARZAN (ATTRIBUTED)

My mom always says, "Keep your chin up."
That's how I ran into the door.

DARYL HOGUE

My mother gave lots of good advice and had a lot to say.
As you get older, you realize everything she said was true.

L E N N Y K R A V I T Z

When something disappointing happened, my mother
would remind me not to let that become my focus.
There's still so much to be grateful for.

K A T H E R I N E H E I G L

Things My Mother Taught Me
Anticipation: "Just wait until your father gets home."
Becoming an adult: "If you don't eat your vegetables,
you'll never grow up."
Genetics: "You are just like your father!"
Humor: "When that lawn mower cuts off your toes, don't
come running to me."
Logic: "If you fall off that swing and break your neck, you
can't go to the store with me."

A N O N Y M O U S

You cannot shake hands with a clenched fist.

I N D I R A G A N D H I

Winning that first game was so important; my mother always said that the first game of the second set was the chance to keep it going if you were ahead or change things if you were behind.

TRACY AUSTIN

You cannot make your decisions based on criticisms. You have to do what you think is right.

ROSALYNN SMITH CARTER

Always be smarter than the people who hire you.

LENA HORNE

When you cease to make a contribution, you begin to die.

ELEANOR ROOSEVELT

If you want your children to turn out well, spend twice as much time with them, and half as much money.

ABIGAIL VAN BUREN

Never allow your child to call you by your first name. He hasn't known you long enough.

FRAN LEBOWITZ

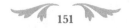

Don't think your kids are going to be less destructive just
because they have a lot of things to entertain them.
We got our kids a swimming pool
and they capsized the house.

PHYLLIS DILLER

Things a Mother Would Never Say
"Let me smell that shirt…
yes, it's good enough for another week."
"Yes, I used to skip school a lot, too."
"Go ahead and keep that stray dog, honey.
I'll be glad to feed and walk him every day."

ANONYMOUS

Never play peek-a-boo with a child on a long plane trip.
There's no end to the game. Finally I grabbed him by the
bib and said, "Look, it's always gonna be me!"

RITA RUDNER

Do not, on a rainy day ask your child what he feels like
doing, because I assure you that what he feels like doing,
you won't feel like watching.

FRAN LEBOWITZ

Never have more children than you have car windows.

E R M A   B O M B E C K

Personally, I think any more than two or three kids
is not a family, it's a litter.

T R A C E Y   U L L M A N

As a girl my temper often got out of bounds.
But one day when I became angry at a friend over some
trivial matter, my mother said to me, "Elizabeth, anyone
who angers you conquers you."

E L I Z A B E T H   K E N N E Y

When I was a child, my mother said to me, "If you
become a soldier, you'll be a general. If you become a
monk, you'll end up as the pope." Instead, I became a
painter and wound up as Picasso.

P A B L O   P I C A S S O

Mama exhorted her children at every opportunity to
"jump at the sun." We might not land on the sun, but at
least we would get off the ground.

Z O R A   N E A L E   H U R S T O N

The real menace in dealing with a five-year-old is that in
no time at all you begin to sound like a five-year-old.

JEAN KERR

Cleaning your house while your kids are still growing is
like shoveling the walk before it stops snowing.

PHYLLIS DILLER

There is no way to be a perfect mother, and a million
ways to be a good one.

JILL CHURCHILL

The fastest way to break the cycle of perfectionism
and become a fearless mother is to give up the idea
of doing it perfectly—indeed to embrace uncertainty
and imperfection.

ARIANNA HUFFINGTON

When my kids become wild and unruly,
I use a nice, safe playpen.
When they're finished, I climb out.

ERMA BOMBECK

"Mother Knows Best"
EDNA FERBER

Mothers know best…
but no one ever listens.
BRUCE LANSKY

You Don't Have To Be Jewish (To Be a Jewish Mother)

MY AUNT JESSIE, WHO WAS LIKE A SECOND MOTHER to me, was divorced, raised two kids by herself, and was on welfare. In spite of this, what I remember most about my aunt was her joyous spirit and sense of humor.

Maybe it was her Hungarian fiery heritage. Maybe it was her way of coping with life. Maybe it was one of the few things she had control over when things were difficult. Maybe it was because she was Jewish and steeped in a tradition of laughing through tears.

Whatever it was, my aunt had a Jewish joie d'vivre. Often

she would tell people that she and my mom were in vaud-erville, which they never were. She would joke that they were billed as the "P Sisters"—Irene and Urene.

Aunt Jessie found happiness in bringing joy to others through her cooking and crocheting, and bringing laughs to others too. Every year when she was about to buy me a gift for my birthday she would jokingly ask, "What size handkerchief do you wear?"

When a waitress or a sales clerk called Jessie "honey," my aunt would respond, "Don't call me honey. Honey is only bee poop."

And her tongue-in-cheek advice to her daughter, Bernice, was, "If a fellow offers to give you a watch, don't accept it. First he'll give you the case then he'll try to give the works."

Probably without knowing it, Aunt Jessie was living her life according to a Jewish saying—"You can't control the wind, but can adjust the sails."

And she did it through ups and downs, as we all can, Jewish or not, with a sense of humor.

Q: How many Jewish mothers does it take
to change a light bulb?
A: "It's all right…I'll sit in the dark."

ANONYMOUS

My mother should have been Jewish.
She could have taught a class on how to induce guilt.

LORNA LUFT

My mother could make anyone feel guilty—
she used to get letters of apology
from people she didn't even know.

JOAN RIVERS

My mother has gossip dyslexia.
She has to talk in front of people's backs.

RICHARD LEWIS

My mother just wrote her autobiography.
Pick it up. It's in the stores right now.
It's entitled I Came, I Saw, I Criticized.

JUDY GOLD

Mama (to grown son on the telephone):
I sat by the phone all day Friday, all day Saturday, and
all day Sunday. Your father said to me, "Phyllis, eat something; you'll faint." I said, "No, Harry, no, I don't want my
mouth to be full when your son calls me."

ELAINE MAY AND MIKE NICHOLS

My mother phones daily to ask, "Did you just try to reach
me?" When I reply, "No," she adds, "So, if you're not too
busy, call me while I'm still alive," and hangs up.

ERMA BOMBECK

I got on the phone, my mom said,
"Hi! Is everything wrong?"

RICHARD LEWIS

Instead of saying "hello," my mother gets on the phone
and says, "Guess who died?"

DOM IRRERA

If mama ain't happy, ain't nobody happy.

ANONYMOUS

I should have realized what was in store for me when my mother tried to stop the obstetrician from cutting the umbilical cord. She argued it was a good way to keep me from getting lost. He cut it off anyway. So she asked for a doggie bag. She still keeps the cord in her drawer. Every now and then she gives it a twist, and I call home.

R. STEVEN ARNOLD

Did you ever meet a mother who's complained that her child phoned her too often?
Me neither.

MAUREEN LIPMAN

My mother says she just wants me to be happy—just doing what she wants me to do.

JULIA WILLIS

As long as I have food and remote control, I'm happy.

MARGIE KLEIN (AUTHOR'S MOTHER)

If my mother knew I did this for a living, she'd kill me. She thinks I'm selling dope.

HENNY YOUNGMAN

My mother. What can I say about such a wonderful,
loving, and caring woman? She kept busy all day
cleaning, cooking, and killing...mainly chickens.
On Friday nights anything with feather was a goner.
That woman plucked till dawn.

MEL BROOKS

My mom is a neat freak. If she adopted a highway, she'd
mop it once a week. She'd reroute traffic: "Don't drive on
my clean freeway!"

DANIEL LIEBERT

My mom is a clean freak. She vacuumed so much,
the guy downstairs went bald.

STEVE BRIDGES

My mother from time to time puts on her wedding dress.
Not because she's sentimental. She just gets really far
behind in her laundry.

BRIAN KILEY

My mother is so neurotic. She puts down toilet paper on
the seat even at our relative's house, at the dinner table.

WENDY LIEBMAN

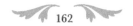

You want to hear the childhood daredevil stories my mother tells company? "Once a glass broke on the kitchen floor, not one week later my daughter was in there without her shoes on." I broke a glass in 1954, they sold the house in 1985, my mother warned the new owners, "I think I got all the big pieces, but there could be slivers."

ELAYNE BOOSLER

There's something wrong with a mother who washes out a measuring cup with soap and water after she's only measured water in it.

ERMA BOMBECK

I found out why cats drink out of the toilet. My mother told me it's because it's cold in there. And I'm like: How did my mother know that?

WENDY LIEBMAN

My mom buys paper plates, three hundred in a big plastic bag. We could take one out whenever we need one, but the rule is we always have to put the twist tie back on the bag. I guess it's to keep them fresh. Nothing ruins my lunch more than a stale paper plate.

JORDAN BRADY

After my brother and I moved out of the house, our mom got a job at a major household appliance company as a customer service representative. On her first day, she got an urgent call from a socialite who complained that she was having an important dinner party that night and her dishwasher, with all her dirty dishes in it, was not working. The woman insisted that a repairman be sent immediately. Mom told the irate customer that it was impossible; the repairman could not be there until the next day.

The woman then shouted, "And what am I supposed to do? I have twelve people coming for dinner tonight and I don't have a clean plate in the house."

Mom replied: "Use paper plates."

That was her first and last day on the job.

ALLEN KLEIN

My mom was a little weird. When I was little Mom would
make chocolate frosting, and she'd let me lick the
beaters. And then she'd turn them off.

MARTY COHEN

A Freudian slip is when you say one thing
but mean your mother.

ANONYMOUS

When my mother had to get dinner for eight she'd just
make enough for sixteen and only serve half.

GRACIE ALLEN

Did you hear about the homeless man
who walked up to a Jewish mother on the street and said,
"Lady, I haven't eaten in three days."
"Force yourself," she replied.

ANONYMOUS

My mother gets all mad at me if I stay in a hotel. I'm
31-years-old, and I don't want to sleep on a sleeping bag
down in the basement. It's humiliating.

BEN AFFLECK

My mom has reached the point where she is so immersed in her own health miseries; she has little patience for any of my problems. One day when I was complaining to her about something that happened to me as "the worst feeling in the world," she shot back: "Worst feeling in the world? Try going without a bowel movement for ten days."

JAN KING

Now Mom's reached the point in her life where she doesn't care what people think. She has a bumper sticker on her car that says: "Honk, if your husband's watching TV and your oldest son doesn't know what he's doing, the other two are in California and New York, one's gay, your daughter's divorced, and you forgot to buy milk while at the store."

BOB SMITH

My mom thinks coupons are money and gives them for gifts.

JAYNE WARREN

Even a secret agent can't lie to a Jewish mother.

PETER MALKIN

We'd ask [my mother] what she wanted for her birthday.
Every year she'd say the same thing. "What do I want for
my birthday? I want you kids to get along.
All I want is peace in the house."
Well, we saved a lot of money on gifts.
JUDY GOLD

My mom is very possessive. She calls me up and says, "You
weren't home last night. Is something going on?" I said,
"Yeah, Mom. I'm cheating on you with another mother."
HEIDI JOYCE

Little Marvin heard a news story on television and rushed
into the kitchen where his mother was preparing dinner.
"Mama, Mama! They said on TV there's going to be an
eclipse! Can I go out and watch?"
"Go darling," said Mama,
"But I'm warning you...don't get too close."
ANONYMOUS

Seymour excitedly told his mother he'd fallen in love and was getting married.

"Mama, just for fun, I'll bring over three women and you guess which one she is." Mama agreed.

The next day Seymour brought over three beauties, who sat on the sofa and chatted with Mama over some tea.

When they left, he said, "O.K., Mama. Guess which one I'm going to marry?"

Without a moment's hesitation, she replied, "The one in the middle with the red hair."

"You're right. But Mama…how did you know?" asked Seymour, amazed.

"Her, I don't like."

ANONYMOUS

I had a Jewish delivery:
they knock you out with the first pain;
they wake you up when the hairdresser shows.

JOAN RIVERS

My parents come from Brooklyn, which is the
heart of the Old World. They're very stable, down-to-
earth people who don't approve of divorce.
Their values in life are God and carpeting.
I came home on a Sunday.... And I said I had to get a
divorce. My mother put down her knitting. She got up
and she went over to the furnace. She opened the door
and she got in. Took it rather badly I thought.

WOODY ALLEN

Three mothers—a Catholic, Polly; a Protestant, Judith;
and Sheila, a Jew—were discussing when life begins.
Polly said: "In our religion, life begins at conception."
Judith said: "In our religion, we believe that life begins
when the fetus is viable away from the mother's womb."
"You're both wrong," said Sheila. "In our religion, life
begins when the kids graduate college and the dog dies."

ANONYMOUS

Susan, forty-three and not married, calls her mother.

"Hello, Ma? It's Susan. Listen, I have some news for you."

"Susan, is that you? Are you O.K.? What's the news?"

"Well, Ma, it finally happened. I met a man. I'm going to get married."

"Susan! That's wonderful darling. I was afraid you never would. Wonderful news. We're so happy for you."

"Ma, before I bring my fiancé to visit, I want to tell you a few things about him. I know this may be hard for you, but he's not of our faith."

"A non-Jew? Nu, it's not so terrible. As we get older, it's important to find somebody, anybody, to build a life with."

"Ma, I knew you would understand. It's great

that we can talk openly to each other. There's another thing I want to tell you. He's not of our color either."

"So…color, shmolor. It doesn't matter. As long as you're happy, then we're happy."

"Ma? You're such a wonderful mother. I feel I can really share things with you. There's one more thing. We don't have enough money to get a place to live."

"Don't worry. When you get married, you'll live with us. You and your new husband can sleep in the master bedroom. And your father will sleep on the couch."

"But, Ma, what about you? Where will you sleep?"

"Honey, about me you shouldn't worry. As soon as I get off the phone, I'm going to stick my head in the oven!"

ANONYMOUS

HISTORICAL MOM'S FAMOUS LAST WORDS

Gandhi's Mom:
"Eat something. You're skin and bones."

Ben Franklin's Mom:
"Get inside and quit playing with that cocka-mamie kite!"

Dr. Jekyll/Mr. Hyde's Mom:
"What's wrong? You don't seem like yourself today."

David Copperfield's Mom:
"You're getting on my nerves. Why don't you just disappear for a while?"

Napoleon Bonaparte's Mom:
"For the last time—get your hands out of your pockets!"

JAN KING

INDEX TO AUTHORS

ABOUT THE AUTHOR

ALLEN KLEIN is an award-winning professional speaker and bestselling author. His first book, *The Healing Power of Humor,* which is now in its fortieth printing and ninth foreign language translation, perfectly sums up his life-long philosophy—that humor is the best medicine for all ailments, big and small. A recipient of a Lifetime Achievement Award from the Association for Applied and Thera-peutic Humor and an inductee into the Hunter College, New York City, Hall of Fame, Allen is also the world's only certified Jollytologist®, earning a Master's Degree from St. Mary's College in humor—no kidding! Nicknamed the "King of Whimsy," Allen has even worked in television production, designing children's television shows at CBS, including the beloved and wildly popular *Captain Kangaroo*, as well as *The Merv Griffin Show* and *The Jackie Gleason Show*. The author of eighteen uplifting and inspiring books, Allen currently resides and writes in San Francisco.

For more information about his books and presentations, go to www.allenklein.com or contact him at allen@allen-klein.com.

To Our Readers

Viva Editions publishes books that inform, enlighten, and entertain. We do our best to bring you, the reader, quality books that celebrate life, inspire the mind, revive the spirit, and enhance lives all around. Our authors are practical visionaries: people who offer deep wisdom in a hopeful and helpful manner. Viva was launched with an attitude of growth and we want to spread our joy and offer our support and advice where we can to help you live the Viva way: vivaciously!

We're grateful for all our readers and want to keep bringing you books for inspired living. We invite you to write to us with your comments and suggestions, and what you'd like to see more of. You can also sign up for our online newsletter to learn about new titles, author events, and special offers.

Viva Editions
2246 Sixth St.
Berkeley, CA 94710
www.vivaeditions.com
(800) 780-2279
Follow us on Twitter @vivaeditions
Friend/fan us on Facebook